Playing with the Past

Playing with the Past

Exploring Values in Heritage Practice

Kate Clark

berghahn

NEW YORK · OXFORD

www.berghahnbooks.com

First published in 2019 by
Berghahn Books
www.berghahnbooks.com

Library of Congress Cataloging-in-Publication Data

Names: Clark, Kate, author.
Title: Playing with the Past: Exploring Values in Heritage Practice / Kate Clark.
Description: New York: Berghahn Books, 2019. | Includes bibliographical references and index.
Identifiers: LCCN 2019013570 (print) | LCCN 2019015963 (ebook) | ISBN 9781789203011 (ebook) |
     ISBN 9781789203127 (hardback: alk. paper) | ISBN 9781789203004 (pbk.: alk. paper)
Subjects: LCSH: Cultural property—Protection—Study and teaching. | Historic preservation—Study
     and teaching.
Classification: LCC CC135 (ebook) | LCC CC135 .C486 2019 (print) | DDC 363.6/90071—dc23
LC record available at https://lccn.loc.gov/2019013570

British Library Cataloguing in Publication Data

A catalogue record for this book is available from the British Library

ISBN 978-1-78920-312-7 hardcover
ISBN 978-1-78920-300-4 paperback
ISBN 978-1-78920-301-1 ebook

CONTENTS

Time spent in reconnaissance is seldom wasted.
—British army saying

What is aught, but as 'tis valued.
—Shakespeare

The better you understand something, the easier it is to change it.
—Allies + Morrison Architects

It's ten years later and people are still asking about how to value culture.
—John Holden, cultural thinker

A right to a heritage brings with it a duty to respect that of others.
—Faro Convention, Council of Europe

Eventually everything connects – people, ideas, objects . . . the quality of the connections is the key to quality per se.
Don't be like I was. Don't be afraid of history. Take all of it you can get.
—Charles Eames, furniture designer

ACTIONS

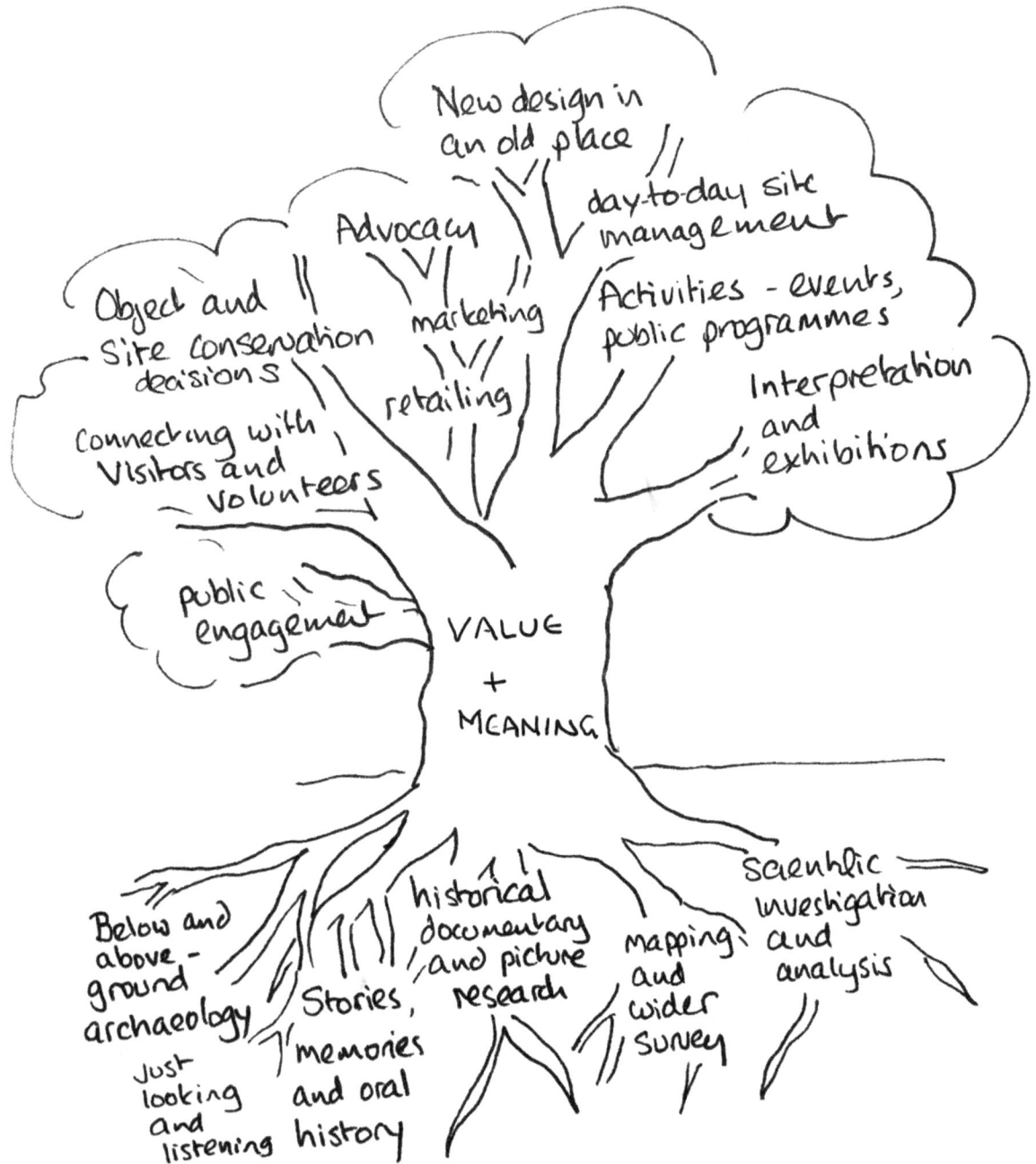

New design in
an old place

day-to-day site
management

Advocacy

Activities - events,
public programmes

Object and
Site conservation
decisions

marketing

Interpretation
and
exhibitions

retailing

Connecting with
visitors and
volunteers

public
engagement

VALUE
+
MEANING

Below and
above-
ground
archaeology

historical
documentary
and picture
research

scientific
investigation
and
analysis

mapping
and
wider
survey

Stories,

Just
looking
and
listening

memories
and oral
history

STORIES

PREFACE

This book is designed to 'train the trainers'. It contains a series of activities that teachers, facilitators and others can use to help students develop the thinking skills they will need in their future heritage practice. It can also be used outside the classroom by anyone who works with heritage and needs to engage with people in order to understand what is important to them and plan for the future. Together these activities provide a toolkit of ideas that can be adapted to the myriad different aspects of managing and caring for anything that matters to people.

The activities are designed to be used by anyone who grapples with the day-to-day complexities of managing historic things or places that are important. That includes people in professions who deal with heritage, such as conservators, museum curators, architects, archaeologists, scientists, anthropologists, surveyors, landscape specialists and historians. It also includes people with specialist cultural knowledge, including community representatives or spokespeople, tribal leaders and members of cultural groups.

It is not an introduction to the academic study of heritage – it is assumed that the users of this book will already have a good working knowledge of the basics of heritage practice, based on their own experience and specialist knowledge. Nor is it a book for university students looking for critical approaches to heritage studies – that is covered better elsewhere.

Instead the activities illustrate and involve 'heritage practice' – the things that organizations (and indeed individuals) do to hand on what matters to them to future generations. Heritage practice is very broad. As well as the basic physical work to care for things and places, it includes activities such as research, conservation, maintenance and repair, planning, decision-making, community engagement, interpretation, site management, designation, advocacy and organizational leadership.

Many different organizations or groups of people are involved in heritage practice. Any organization that deals with heritage, including museums, public and private sector bodies as well as voluntary groups, will deal with some or all of these issues. However, it is not just heritage organizations that are involved with heritage practice. There are many other groups and organizations who are responsible for heritage assets, even though it is not their primary purpose; they too need to include heritage practice as part of what they do.

The philosophical approach that underpins the activities can best be described as 'values-based' heritage practice. In short, this approach takes the view that what defines heritage is its value to people, and therefore understanding that value is central to finding ways to sustain it for the future.

Values-based practice recognizes that over the past few decades heritage policy has been changing and moving from 'push' to 'pull' – to a world where heritage specialists are facilitators and not dictators who recognize that unless they are sensitive to and engaged with people and what is important to them it is very difficult to conserve things in the long run. This does not displace the need for good technical conservation or management skills but works with them.

It is a book to be used rather than read. Each activity is designed to inspire thinking and debate. Users will want to mix and match activities in order to put together their own events, workshops or courses, tailored to specific circumstances, and drawing on their own experience and knowledge. But whilst users might select individual activities, I hope that taken together, these activities form a useful, practical tool-kit that illustrates the basic tenets of values-based practice in heritage.

Over time, I hope that these activities will adapt and evolve as people find new ways to explore and tease out that delightful, frustrating, elusive complexity that is the value people place on their cultural heritage and the challenge of passing it on to the future.

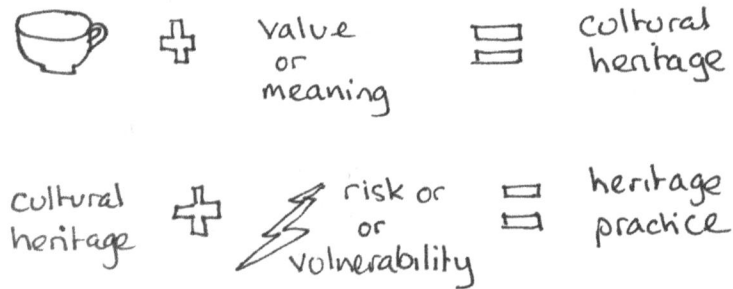

ORIGINS AND INSPIRATIONS

Traditionally, heritage specialists have used their expertise to define the significance of heritage sites, but increasingly practitioners will need to behave less like dictators and more like facilitators – listening to people, engaging with communities and helping groups to explore what matters, rather than telling them. Yet most of us were not taught how to do this. These activities are a series of practical ways to help involve people in the kinds of day-to-day thinking that anyone who looks after heritage needs to do, such as business planning, developing new interpretation, commercial development, operational site management or advocacy.

I started using activities in the 1990s in the UK to help community groups think about heritage values. A new fund had been set up to support heritage (the Heritage Lottery Fund, now the National Lottery Heritage Fund), with a clear philosophy of enabling communities to care for what mattered to them. The fund had a very broad remit and could support everything from museums and biodiversity to industrial heritage, archives and archaeology.

The fund did not use experts to define heritage but asked applicants themselves to put forward a convincing case for why their heritage was important. In order to do this, applicants were asked to prepare 'Conservation Management Plans' with 'Statements of Significance' at their core. It soon became clear that most of these plans were written by experts with a good technical knowledge of heritage but few skills in community engagement. No one had talked to the people who cared most about the site about why it mattered to them, and yet they were the people who would be involved in looking after it in the long run.

As an antidote, I created 'The Big Picture' activity (see Section 3) to bring together community groups in order to understand why heritage mattered to them. By articulating different views and writing them down, it meant that community perspectives could be fed into the overall management plan and, more importantly, be taken into account in thinking about the future of the site. 'The Big Picture' was a great way to structure a discussion about value, and I used it as a basis for workshops involving a wide range of people, from tenants at a social housing estate to the Dean and Chapters of various Cathedrals, and from First Nations groups in Canada to communities in Hungary.

The values-based approach to heritage can be used across the world, regardless of specific heritage legislation or policy. Although it was perhaps first articulated in the Australian 'Burra Charter', it can be applied anywhere. I learned this as part of the Getty Conservation Institute (GCI) values project, where staff from the US Parks Service, English Heritage, Parks Canada and Australia looked at how values underpinned decision-making. Despite different legal and policy approaches, the idea of significance and value lies at the heart of any heritage process.

These activities might never have gone any further had it not been for the 'HLF Way', a day of games and activities created by the then policy team to train staff to assess grant applications and make good recommendations. They illustrated other aspects of the HLF philosophy – putting communities in the driving seat, embedding access and learning into all projects, and assessing the quality of business planning. The day inspired me to think more widely about the use of games and activities in heritage learning.

Several years later, I was asked to teach students from Zimbabwe, Ethiopia, Ghana, Kenya and South Africa on the Robben Island heritage management course. I set myself the challenge of using as few lectures as possible – our classroom was the World Heritage Site around us, with its opportunities and genuine management challenges. The students road-tested lots of the activities but also helped me develop new ones. Our discussions kept coming back to the link between heritage and identity in a way that was very different to the way that students in the UK talk about heritage. As a result, I was inspired to begin this book with activities that focus on the role of heritage in individual identity.

The activities that focus on economic and social values, public value and benefit were inspired by another important initiative in values-based thinking – the 'Public Value of Heritage' project with colleagues from the Heritage Lottery Fund, English Heritage and the National Trust. We needed to demonstrate the value of the huge investment the fund had made in heritage, so we worked with John Holden and Robert Hewison to find ways to capture that. A range of experts debated the idea of public value at a major conference in London in 2006. Although the papers from the conference have been published, I created the activities around evaluation, public value and advocacy as a way of making 'Public Value' more readily accessible.

The practical on-site activities were inspired by the many guides, custodians and site staff I have worked with at Ironbridge Gorge Museums, Sydney Living Museums and at Cadw, the Welsh Government's Historic Environment service. I wanted to capture and share some of the unsung skills involved in the day-to-day management of heritage sites, where one person is often dealing with everything from retailing, interpretation and customer service to blocked gutters and health and safety. The best heritage managers are often those on the front desk of the museum or site because their job is to connect people with heritage. Some of the best contributions to values workshops and planning days have come from people on the front line.

Another key influence was the branding project that we undertook with Frost Design at the Historic Houses Trust of NSW. In the process of exploring new ways to connect audiences with historic house museums, I learned that rebranding an organization is not simply a design exercise but a way to understand the core values of the organization. In effect, we were creating a 'statement of significance' for a set of museums. It inspired me to think further about how understanding history, memory and identity can not only help in managing places and things – it has relevance to organizations as a whole and inspired some of the activities in the section on heritage organizations.

The National Trust's 'Spirit of Place' work has been another inspiration. 'Spirit of Place' makes a strong connection between heritage values and wider site management issues such as marketing and interpretation. I have included 'Spirit of Place' as one of the activities, but the concept has also helped to inform some of the other activities in this book.

The important thing is that these activities continue to evolve. Some I have played hundreds of times; others just a few times, and some have been created in the process of putting together this book. Each is based on a core heritage concept in heritage management and on practical experience in looking after museums and heritage sites. However, the details of how the activities should be played and what works best in different settings can't always be anticipated when setting them down on paper. I would welcome feedback from anyone doing these activities in order to help refine them.

Activities such as these are like storytelling – essentially an oral tradition. They can be written down, but this simply captures them at a moment in time. I hope they will develop a life of their own – growing and improving over time as others use them.

ACKNOWLEDGEMENTS AND THANKS

This book draws on the work of a wide range of other people. 'Our Neighbourhood, Our Map' and 'The Professor of Archaeology' are broadly based on activities in Chris Johnson's *House of Games* (1998). 'An Encounter with the Past – Learning and Feeling', 'Vote for My Interpretation Project!' and the 'History Lucky Dip – The Meaning of Objects' were part of the original 'HLF Way' course developed by Jo Reilly, Karen Brookfield, Sharon Goddard, Sheena Vick, Catherine Ware, and Gareth Maeer. Sarah Staniforth and the team at the National Trust of England and Wales created the 'Spirit of Place' and the associated worksheets, and I want to thank her for permission to use them; Cat Burgess at Frost Design used 'My Best Day Out' at a workshop for Sydney Living Museums; Sharon Sullivan inspired the 'Bad Fairy' exercise ('... And Who Needs to Be Involved?'); Professor Mark Moore used the example of the police in a lecture about public value which I adapted as the 'Public Value of Heritage' activity; Alison Crowther showed me the carousel technique and other basic facilitation techniques; Danny Burchill and colleagues played museum games at the Museums Association conference in Cardiff in 2014 and inspired 'Be Creative – Devise a Museum Game!'. 'Bureaucrat Bootcamp', the mock hearing, is based on a course Malcolm Airs ran at the Oxford Department for Continuing Education. At the University of Pennsylvania, I watched Don Rypkema challenge his students to think like local mayors and developers – hence 'Two Minutes in the Lift with the Mayor'. 'Scrutinize your Business Plan' is based on an activity by Ian Morrison and Gareth Maeer.

Henrietta Clark helped turn this manuscript from a tangled mass into something with structure and direction, and Cornelius Holtorf provided very helpful feedback. Others who have contributed to these activities and my thinking about heritage (either directly or indirectly) include Andrew Acland, Judith Alfrey, Kay Andrews, John Barnes, Ian Baxter, Karen Brookfield, Andy Brown, Kristal Buckley, Caroline Butler-Bowdon, Christina Cameron, John Carman, Chris Catling, Judy Cligman, Harriet Deacon, Boris Deanovic, Paul Drury, Keith Emerick, John Fidler, Jim Gard'ner, David Heath, Mark Horton, Gwilym Hughes, Chris Johnston, Toshiyuku Kono, Susan MacDonald, Richard Mackay, Randy Mason, Michael Rose, Henry Russell, Kylie Seretis, George Smith, Hilary Soderland, Steve Trow, Robin Turner, Alexandra Warr, Chris Young, David Worth and the team at the Getty Conservation Institute. I still miss talking to four particular inspirations – Ian Constantinides, Michael Stratton, Joan Kerr and James Semple Kerr. My biggest thanks go to Owen, Hetty and Jack, who above all, have taught me to play. This is for them.

Because activities such as these are often – like the best oral traditions – handed down from one practitioner to another, it is not always easy to identify or acknowledge the original author. If I have inadvertently used something in this book without proper acknowledgement, do please let me know.

INTRODUCTION

This introduction provides more detail on the approach to heritage used in this book, including common terms that cut across different types of natural and cultural heritage and how to use the activities.

Everybody has a heritage. We all have stories, language, places and things – whether natural or cultural – that have shaped who we are and how we see the world. Some of those are important enough for us to want to hand them on as a legacy to future generations – whether to our own children or to the wider community.

Looking after heritage is something that we do in our own lives when we take photographs or pass on traditions or save things in a trunk in the attic. But it is also something that societies do collectively in identifying heritage assets – those things that matter to a wider group of people that are part of the common good.

Defining that heritage – why it matters and to whom – is no easy matter, especially when doing so on a collective basis. Intervening in heritage has both the power to do good and also to do harm, to bring people together and to divide them.

But the starting point for all heritage activity is understanding what matters to people and why. The activities in this book are all designed to help those who deal with heritage to understand and to help articulate what people value and why it is important to them, and to use that knowledge to inform the things we need to do to hand it on to future generations.

Because the activities in the book are relevant to many different types of heritage and many different areas of knowledge, some common terms have been adopted. The intention is not to undermine the language or expertise used by any particular heritage sector but simply to avoid long lists explaining all of the different types of heritage that an activity might be relevant to.

Most of the activities in the book also have a common underlying theme – different ways of exploring how and why people value heritage and using that understanding to help shape decisions and other heritage activities. Again, this is something that is relevant to every different type of heritage in one way or another.

HERITAGE ASSETS

Throughout this book, the generic term 'heritage asset' is used to refer to something that we might consider to be part of the heritage. There are many different definitions of heritage, but for the purposes of the activities in this book, the definition of a heritage asset is:

Anything that we value collectively and want to hand on to the future.

That definition includes both physical things (tangible heritage) and intangible heritage.

Physical or tangible heritage includes:

- historic buildings, sites, monuments and places
- historic items or collections, including works of art, archives, industrial items
- landscapes, parks and gardens
- species, biodiversity and natural heritage
- historic infrastructure such as canals, railways and bridges etc.

Intangible heritage can be just as important as tangible heritage. Intangible heritage assets are those things that we want to hand on to future generations that don't necessarily have a physical form, such as:

- languages
- skills including craftsmanship and knowledge
- stories and memories
- traditions including food and farming
- music, dance, ceremonies and other activities

Any of these intangible forms of heritage may also be captured in physical form in books, archives, photographs, video and other records, which people may want to preserve.

HERITAGE PRACTICE

Handing heritage assets on to future generations involves doing something to prolong their life, often over and beyond their original purpose, or in the face of rapid change or loss. Prolonging the life of something important involves many different actions. For example, caring for assets includes the technical work needed to repair, restore, reinstate or reintroduce heritage, as well other kinds of preservation, such as digital preservation. Associated with this are activities such as understanding and researching heritage, scientific investigation, the process of selecting, planning and decision-making around heritage assets, new design and architecture in natural or cultural landscapes or historic places, or repair and restoration in art. Even intangible heritage can be preserved to some extent through recordings, digitization and appropriate data standards.

But heritage practice is as much a social discipline as a technical one. It involves engaging with people to understand heritage or to enable people to enjoy, learn about, share or transmit to to the future heritage. Activities such as maintaining traditional knowledge, as well as language skills, education, interpretation and exhibitions, citizen science, marketing and community engagement, all play a role in sustaining heritage.

Business activities are also part of heritage practice, such as income generation, finding new uses for assets, governance and leadership in heritage organizations. Economics, social and health sciences and environmental sciences help us to understand the economic, social and environmental benefits of heritage.

Doing nothing can also contribute to heritage practice – not demolishing a building, throwing away an artefact, ploughing a field or developing a site are also ways of helping to ensure things are there in the future, as can be keeping traditional knowledge secret.

WELL WE FINALLY GOT IT REPAIRED, BUT WHAT ARE WE GOING TO DO WITH IT ??

Once again there are many different terms used to describe the process of doing all of this. Words like 'sustainability', 'conservation', 'preservation', 'restoration', 'cultural resource management', 'heritage management', 'designation', 'protection' and more. For some types of heritage, these words have very specific meanings – archival practice, for example, differentiates 'conservation' and 'preservation', whereas other disciplines or countries might use the same word in different ways.

Because the activities in this book are relevant to any kind of heritage, the neutral term 'heritage practice' has been adopted as a shorthand for all of the different activities involved in caring for heritage assets. 'Heritage practice' as used here includes the two related areas of work – understanding and caring for (conserving or preserving) heritage assets and engaging with people in and around heritage in order to sustain it for the future.

Within heritage practice, there is a distinction between what might be described as 'formal' and 'informal' heritage practice. Formal or public heritage practice – sometimes known as 'authorized heritage practice' – comprises those things that are undertaken by heritage organizations or agencies, on behalf of, and often with the involvement of, the public and within the framework of legal or democratic

OPERATIONAL
Project delivery
Site management
Visitor services
Organisational leadership

LEGAL
Designation
regulation
Policy

FINANCIAL
Grants, subsidies
Incentives

TECHNICAL
Craft skills
Conservation +
repair techniques
maintenance

POLITICAL
Advocacy, influencing
social media
campaigning
marketing

PEOPLE-BASED
Listening + storytelling
Co-production
audience focus
partnership
access + participation
compassion

EVIDENTIAL
Academic research
Policy research + evaluation
Survey + investigation
data + information
traditional knowledge

FORMAL HERITAGE PRACTICE

accountability to elected representatives. It might include designation or the selection of heritage assets for protection or inclusion in a museum, the allocation of funding or use of tax incentives, the management of parks or public lands or providing specialist advice within the land-use planning system. Formal heritage practice also includes things like legal requirements, codes of conduct or professional standards.

Informal heritage practice comprises the many other things that people do to look after heritage, whether in their own lives or as an incidental part of their work or other activities. Family history, recording bird species, genealogy, creating a website, gardening, telling stories to grandchildren or putting together an exhibition or book are some of the many examples of informal heritage practice. All of them result in something that enables knowledge or heritage assets to be passed on in some way.

PRACTITIONERS AND SPECIALISTS

Another challenge that arose in compiling this book was explaining who it is for. At one level, anyone can engage with or care about heritage, whether it is the environment, their family, their local area, their home or their culture. Someone researching their family history is engaging with their heritage using archives, records and memories (informal heritage practice).

But there are also many different people and professions who specialize in heritage or whose special skills and knowledge contribute to safeguarding it, often but not always as part of formal heritage practice. For example:

- community leaders, tribal groups, First Nations and others who are keepers of traditional knowledge and both tangible and intangible heritage
- planners, architects, surveyors, designers and others who deal with historic places, sites and buildings
- ecologists, scientists, farmers, landowners and others who deal with natural and landscape heritage
- curators and other museums professionals, archivists and others who deal with historic items and collections
- consultants from many different disciplines who advise others on heritage assets, management or projects

Because of the diversity of what constitutes heritage, and the many different areas of work that contribute to heritage practice, the term 'heritage specialists' is used to refer to people with a special expertise in one area or more of heritage. Heritage specialists also include those with the technical skills involved in looking after heritage, from traditional buildings skills, species identification and skills in the conservation of materials such as paper to the practical skills involved in archaeology, historical research, or anthropology and the various sciences involved in conserving heritage assets. In the academic sector, there are those who specialize in heritage, landscape, conservation and museum studies, as well as so many other disciplines that touch upon heritage, from architecture through to zoology. Community elders or leaders will also have a special expertise in heritage.

The term 'specialist' is used here over the word 'expert' to reflect the changing nature of heritage practice. Traditionally, heritage experts have taken a lead role in determining what matters and why. Today that knowledge remains vital – but it often contributes to only one part of the many different ways in which heritage is valued. Heritage experts tell others what matters – heritage specialists combine their own skills and knowledge with the ability to also understand, respect, help articulate and work with the values of others.

It is also useful to understand the different groups and organizations that are involved in heritage practice. For some, heritage practice is their primary purpose. Museums, community groups or organizations who look after heritage sites and collections and open them to the public are easily identified as 'heritage organizations', as are those who regulate heritage as part of their wider role, such as local, state and national governments, as well as voluntary bodies, charities and international bodies who advocate for heritage.

But beyond this core group are many other bodies who are responsible for heritage, although it is not their primary purpose. Examples include faith groups, the military, schools and universities, hotels or other businesses. Those bodies may be community groups or in the voluntary, public or private sector. They are involved in heritage practice either because they own, manage, use or occupy a heritage asset, or because their activities have an impact on heritage in some way.

HERITAGE VALUES

Values are what people care about. Understanding value lies at the heart of heritage practice – whether formal or informal. Concepts of value underpin choices about what to protect and why, and they also inform the whole process of sustaining or managing heritage assets in order to hand them on to future generations. They are also relevant to how heritage practitioners, and indeed heritage organizations, behave. The activities in this book are designed to explore some of these different values and show how they can be applied in practice.

This book looks at three different kinds of values in heritage practice.

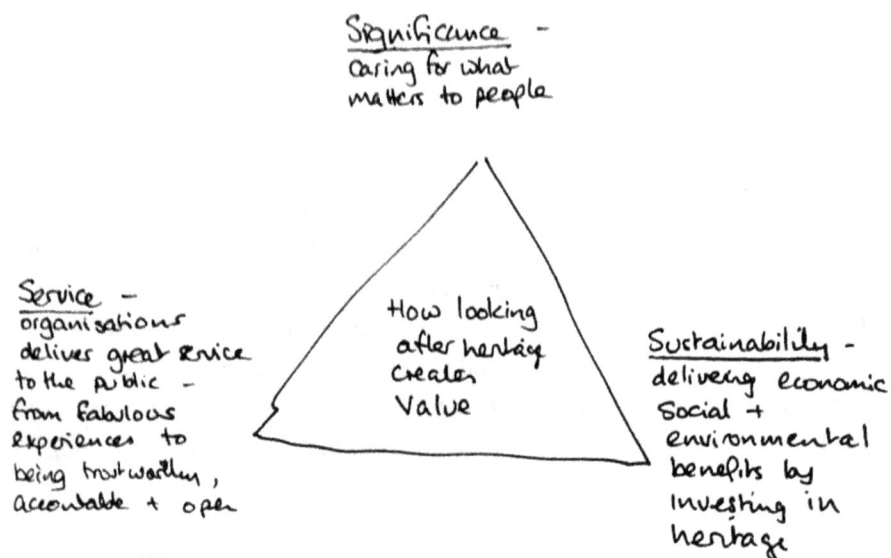

1. The meaning or value of heritage assets (sometimes called significance), which justifies their protection and informs decisions about their future
2. The economic, social and environmental benefits that flow from protecting or caring for heritage assets (sustainability)
3. The values held by heritage organizations or groups, demonstrated in the way they behave and the services they provide for the pubic

Broadly, these relate to the value of what heritage practitioners do, why they do it and how it is done.

Heritage Values ('Significance')

Heritage assets can be important for many different reasons. A species may be rare or endangered, a building may be of architectural or historic importance, an archaeological site may be of potential importance as a source of knowledge. Objects may be beautiful, unusual or exquisite craftsmanship; an industrial site may embody technological innovation. Language, stories and myths may be part of our history and identity and shape the way we see the world.

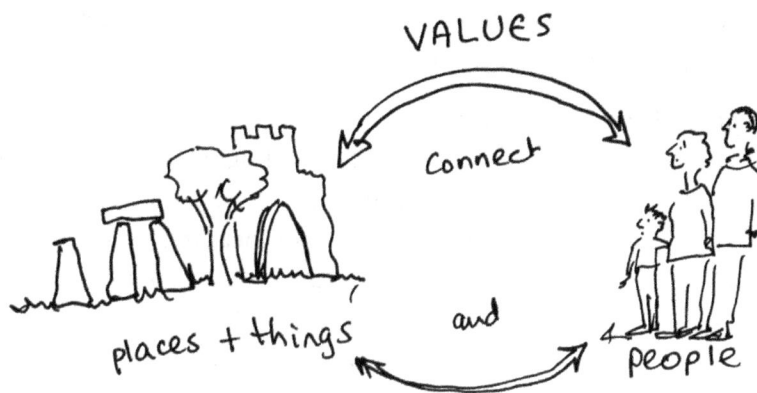

Heritage assets do not have to be old – there are many recent things that we might want to keep for the future. Nor need they be rare – species or buildings that are typical of an area can be important. Heritage assets are not necessarily comfortable – there are difficult places and stories that we want to keep. But in the widest sense, these are all things that matter to us now and that we hope future generations might value, and therefore we look for ways to pass them on.

One of the principal ways in which values are used in formal heritage practice is in the selection of things, sites or areas to protect in law or through the planning system or as a publicly accessible site – such a park, museum or other heritage attraction. The choice of assets for formal protection on behalf of the public is generally known as designation (or registration, listing or scheduling). It involves identifying those assets that meet specific criteria in terms of the type of value and degree of significance.

For example, when a site is put on the World Heritage list it is because it is determined to be of 'Outstanding Universal Value'; when an object is put in a museum it is because of the value we ascribe to it. When a park or building is protected it is because of those values, and when we spend time researching our own history or stories it is because we value them. Other ways of selecting things include museum or archive collections policies.

Most countries, states and some regions have their own regimes and legislation for protecting heritage, and within those contexts different policies or legislation are applied to natural and cultural heritage. There are also international conventions and frameworks relating to natural and cultural heritage. Those systems are all based on some concept of wider public good or collective value for heritage assets, which justifies their protection and imposes a degree of selectivity. This is usually expressed as a set of values. So for built cultural heritage assets that might be protected, these values would typically be archaeological or evidential, architectural, aesthetic, historical or scientific, and they may also be social, spiritual, economic, environmental or something else. For natural heritage, issues such as rarity and biodiversity come into play. There are also broader values around character and distinctiveness, often applied to places that merit protection. Museums, archives and other collections bodies (for example historic ships) will also impose degrees of selectivity on which assets may be protected.

As well as different kinds of values, formal heritage protection often involves levels or degrees of significance; typically, international, national and state levels of significance are used to select assets worthy of protection. Rarity, degree of threat, group value and diversity are also measures of significance. Such measures are used to express the wider collective value of heritage as a basis for a decision about what to protect or where to invest scarce resources. For the purposes of this book, 'significance' is generally used to refer to the degree to which heritage assets matter to people.

The value that people place on heritage often goes well beyond the relatively narrow range of values used in formal heritage practice. Cultural and natural heritage also has value to us as individuals – our culture, environment and heritage contribute to our identity and who we are, and understanding heritage enables us to respect others. Culture and heritage are often at the root of deep-seated conflicts, and the loss of contact with, or erosion of, culture and heritage can have a long-lasting impact on individuals and communities. This is why cultural heritage sites in particular are often specifically targeted at times of war and conflict.

Heritage assets may be of amenity value or communal or spiritual value. They may be fun; they may inspire fear or awe; they may be places to come together or be apart from people.

And those values change. The ways in which people value heritage are not static – they change over time, with knowledge, culture, politics and economics. The activities in this book are designed to tease out different ways in which assets are valued. Although some activities focus on the use of values in designation and protection, many of the others go well beyond that formal list of values.

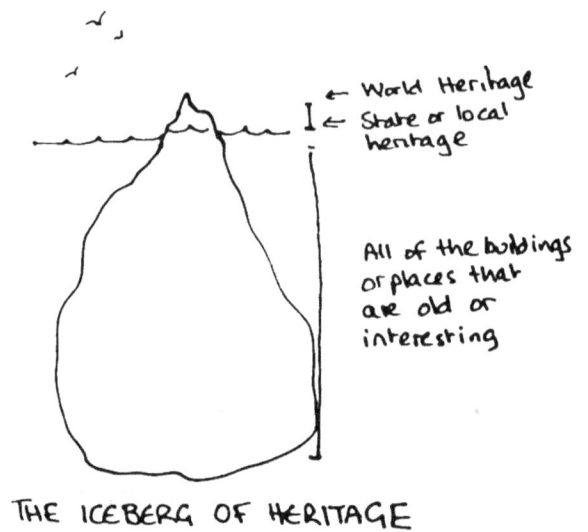

← World Heritage
← State or local heritage

All of the buildings or places that are old or interesting

THE ICEBERG OF HERITAGE

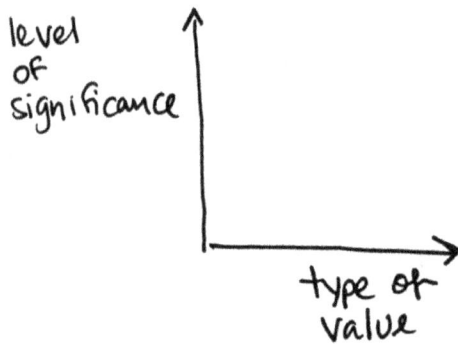

level of significance

type of value

The Benefits of Caring for Heritage ('Sustainability')

As well as the meanings that people ascribe to heritage assets, heritage practice can deliver value in other ways. The many different activities involved in the process of sustaining or caring for heritage assets themselves have the potential to deliver wider benefits for people, over and beyond simply conserving something. In relation to the environment, conserving existing buildings can reduce waste; conserving biodiversity and species contributes to wider environmental benefits; caring for heritage can contribute to the quality of urban and rural environments.

Heritage projects such as exhibitions or activities that involve people can also deliver social benefits. For example, understanding and interpreting heritage can contribute to social inclusion by reflecting different identities and stories. Learning outside the classroom can benefit people of all ages, whilst taking part in heritage activities can be enjoyable, bring mental and physical health benefits or bring people together. There is also a growing body of evidence for the economic benefits of investing in heritage assets, delivering jobs, supporting local businesses and developing skills as well as protecting the amenity value of places where people live.

Note that there are also disbenefits that can arise from poor practice – selecting one kind of heritage over another can leave people feeling disenfranchised, their stories and history excluded. Caring for one kind of heritage might create problems for another kind of heritage – such as the conflicts that can arise between bats and historic buildings.

Articulating the economic, social and environmental benefits that can arise from caring for heritage is particularly helpful in negotiations around whether (or not) to save a heritage asset. It helps to be able to connect heritage to wider agendas and show how caring for heritage can contribute to areas such as economic development, social care or environmental protection.

Values in Heritage Organizations ('Service')

The third kind of value is demonstrated in the way heritage groups or organizations behave – and the service they provide to the public and to others. In terms of behaviour, organizations can demonstrate value through things like transparency and accountability. Areas such as customer service, whether for visitors or others, are hugely important, as is the reputation of heritage organizations, or their ability to demonstrate professional standards. Ethics are also important in many different ways for heritage organizations. Sometimes called 'public value', these values are as relevant to heritage practice as other kinds of values, so there are also activities in the book dealing with issues such as ethics and organizational values.

THE ROLE OF VALUES IN MANAGING CHANGE

Values-based heritage practice recognizes that caring for heritage involves both looking after things and engaging with people. The two are interrelated. At its most basic, managing heritage assets is about managing change. Over time, things change – but whilst we can't always stop or reverse that change, we can sometimes influence it in such a way as to try to preserve what is important to us, for the benefit of future generations. And the way we do that is by understanding what people value and why and using that to shape decision-making. Despite the name, heritage practice is a forward-looking activity that seeks to reconcile the old and the new; to be creative without losing sight of what matters. This approach acknowledges the academic concerns that heritage is a deeply complex and contested space where people have very strong feelings.

In the context of economic development, attempts to protect heritage assets are often caricatured as being backward-looking, stopping progress, creating additional costs and generally being obstructive. Heritage can also be used and manipulated in political and other contexts. The claim that 'we can't protect everything' is often used to denigrate heritage activities. Yet heritage specialists are very aware that change is inevitable – so much of what they seek to do is to help manage change in a way that is sensitive to what people value now.

Change is often resented because it means loss. However, there are ways of planning and delivering change in order to reduce that sense of loss. New neighbourhoods can be designed to combine the familiar and cherished with great new facilities; change in organizations can be managed in a way that builds on the best of what people can and have already achieved, and communities can embrace new cultures without losing sight of traditional values.

The key to managing change is to start by understanding what is there now and why it is important (or not) to people – and only then design change in a way that recognizes both the value of what has been and what could be. It takes time and resources to research the history of a place, to understand organizational values or to appreciate the values of, for example, a different faith. And when there are pressures for change, understanding history and heritage values can seem like a poor use of resources. Yet, ignoring the existing values of place or community (or even organization) can have major cost implications. It may take longer for people to accept change; there may be disputes and appeals, lost productivity, delays and ultimately the new may be worse than the old.

Poorly designed change takes its toll on individuals, on places and organizations. Thus the activities in this book are all designed to help use an understanding of different values as a starting point for managing change – ranging from new developments or making decisions about how best to conserve or restore something, through to finding ways to engage people in history and heritage and to interpret sites. Even the activities that are about specific technical issues such as maintenance recognize that there is value in prioritizing work.

CONFLICTING VALUES

Ultimately, heritage practice is about dealing with or reconciling conflicting values. There may be conflicts between economic, social and environmental values for a place, between the values of different disciplines (e.g. architects, archaeologists) or between different communities (residents, new arrivals) or different knowledge groups (scientists, traditional owners). Rather than shying away from conflicting values, values-based practice embraces

this, putting effort into articulating those different values and finding ways to ideally reconcile them as part of a new design, development or interpretation, or decisions about preservation, funding or regulation. Invariably, matters of conflicting value come down to deeper issues such as power and authority. Here the heritage practitioner may be able to do little more than capture and unravel the stories of a place or object and work with different communities to articulate value in the best way possible, as a starting point for finding ways to reconcile different viewpoints.

TECHNICAL SKILLS VS PEOPLE SKILLS IN HERITAGE

In order to manage change, heritage practice involves engaging with people. For example, some of the people-based activities in heritage practice include:

- citizen science and other ways of involving people in heritage conservation or new developments, such as volunteering, consultation or co-design
- understanding and exploring the heritage of different groups or places
- exhibitions, site interpretation and other ways of reaching people
- public programmes and events at heritage sites or in and around heritage
- training and skills

The technical skills of heritage practice remain absolutely essential, but they sit beside people skills, including the ability to listen, to engage and involve people, or to develop techniques for co-design. Collaboration and working with partners are equally important for heritage practice, as is the ability to engage with different disciplines and different areas.

Equally important is the recognition that heritage can be a difficult and contested place. Heritage has the power to divide people and to bring them together, to exclude and include. Knowing this, heritage practitioners also need to be aware of the potential harm that can result from the way in which we preserve, interpret and manage heritage and be sensitive to the nuances of different versions of the past and indeed the present. Ethics, philosophy, psychology and skills in conflict resolution, mediation and cultural understanding also play a key role in heritage practice.

HOW TO USE THIS BOOK

This is a book to use rather than read. It contains a series of activities that can either be used in day-to-day heritage practice or used to develop skills in heritage practice. Similar activities are used by teachers, leaders, actors, marketers, planners and creative people to help with everything from classroom learning to strategic planning and place-making and community engagement.

These activities began life as an alternative to formal lectures to teach heritage site management. However, it soon became apparent that they had a wider application within heritage practice as ways of structuring community engagement in planning and decision-making and as part of the toolkit for heritage leaders. This book is designed for specialist heritage practitioners who are facing particular challenges in and around working with people to find ways to sustain that heritage. Those challenges might include the need to:

- better understand the views of a community group
- plan for the future of a heritage asset
- train staff or volunteers in heritage organizations
- introduce heritage concepts to non-specialists who have a role in caring for heritage
- develop management or leadership skills in volunteers or professionals
- engage with staff, volunteers or others in strategic planning for organizations
- undertake specific heritage tasks such as putting together a management plan
- bring together different heritage specialists to develop or manage a heritage project

Each activity illustrates a different aspect of heritage practice – such as planning, decision-making, evaluation, advocacy, project or site management, maintenance and more. Some are designed to develop strategic thinking skills; others help tackle practical day-to-day site management. Each has three sections – an aim, a challenge and a discussion to follow. Note that although some could be classed as games, some are not, so the term 'activity' has been used throughout. Some are very brief and require little preparation; others are more complex. Some can be done in a classroom; others are better done on site. Note that if working at a heritage site, you will need to think about logistics; if you are working in a classroom you may also need to prepare materials such as case studies.

The majority of activities can either be used to 'do' something – such as prepare a heritage impact assessment – or to 'teach' those skills. Thus a planner might use an activity to bring together a group to explore the impact of a new proposal on a heritage asset, whilst a trainer might use the same activity to teach generic skills in impact assessment. Where there is a need to 'do' something, it is assumed that the activity will be applied to a particular heritage asset or task – such as developing a management plan or heritage impact assessment for a site. The facilitator might want to gather some information about the asset in advance, but otherwise there is no need for much preparation. However, if the activities are being used in teaching, the facilitator may need to prepare a case study in advance in order to illustrate the heritage technique. For example, if the activity involves developing a statement of significance, they will need to prepare a case study and some background information for the group to use.

The activities can be grouped into workshops or events, which might range from a couple of hours to a full training course. Some are introductory; others are longer activities that may take several hours. They can be combined with more formal presentations, or site visits. These activities are simply ideas. They are not intended to be rigid structures. It is assumed that leaders or facilitators will bring their own specialist knowledge into play but also tailor the activities to meet the requirements of the group, heritage asset or particular challenge.

A Note of Caution

How people value something can be very personal and emotional. Articulating that is in itself an art – words, pictures or some other creative way of expressing ideas are useful to reflect and convey a collective sense of value sensitively. The process may involve making public deeply held views or beliefs and coming close to sharing things that people don't want to share. For this reason, it is important to be sensitive to what people want to share and how. And if you are using values in designation, heritage management or any other formal context, remember that values don't fit easily in boxes or rigid categories. A rigid adherence to some categories of value and the strict exclusion of others can do a great deal of damage not just to heritage but to communities.

PLANNING AND FACILITATING WORKSHOPS

As noted in the introduction, these activities are primarily designed for people who look after heritage in some way, whether professionals, traditional owners, volunteers, or people who come to heritage from other backgrounds.

LOCATION

Some activities are carried out on site; others in a classroom or workspace. For workshops, you will need tables and chairs and to lay the room out accordingly. Avoid university lecture theatres with fixed benches of tiered seating facing forward; huge hotel conference spaces with low ceilings and dark edges are also difficult.

THINK ABOUT THE ROOM LAYOUT

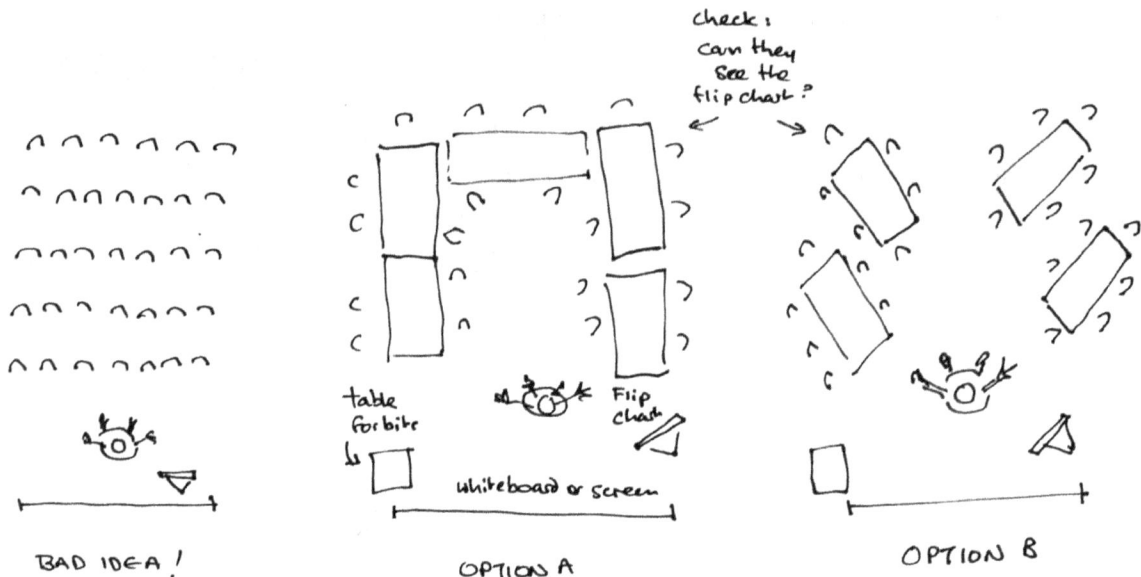

check: can they see the flip chart?

table for bits

Flip chart

whiteboard or screen

BAD IDEA !

OPTION A

OPTION B

SIZE OF GROUP

Around 15–25 people is best – that is large enough to have a variety of different perspectives and small enough to enable everyone to contribute. If there are more than twenty-five people, adapt the activities to reflect that. For example, gather people around tables and adapt the feedback strategies to take one or two points from each table, rather than from each person. The group size will also impact on timings for the day – most of the activities involve feedback, so allow at least 5–7 minutes for any team to feed back an issue. Seat larger groups around individual tables, but don't spread them out too much. Put the flip chart at the front where everyone can see it. It is better if people are seated close together rather than too spread out.

EQUIPMENT

Whilst whiteboards and electronic classroom equipment can be used (if available), I prefer old-fashioned paper and pens because they are easy, flexible, hands-on and immediate.

Almost all these activities assume that you have as standard items at least one flip chart full of paper, a board to write on, such as a whiteboard or blackboard, and marker pens that can be used on paper and/or on a whiteboard. Some venues no longer have these, so do check in advance. Many of the activities also use the following items:

- Post-it notes in different sizes and colours (not the tiny ones)
- lots of spare marker pens, in a variety of colours, for flips charts and whiteboards
- coloured dots or gold stars for ranking things
- Blu-Tack or tape for attaching large pieces of paper to the wall or board
- ideally, a wall that you can stick bits of paper to that won't mark
- scissors, and squares of white card
- a spare pad of A4 paper, and ordinary pens
- a bell or whistle
- a kitchen timer

It is also useful to have a board on which to hang large pieces of paper (some venues do not allow things to be stuck to walls) and a projector and laptop if a case study is needed. If the workshop needs to be written up afterwards, use a camera or mobile phone to photograph any notes and even the event in progress if participants consent to it.

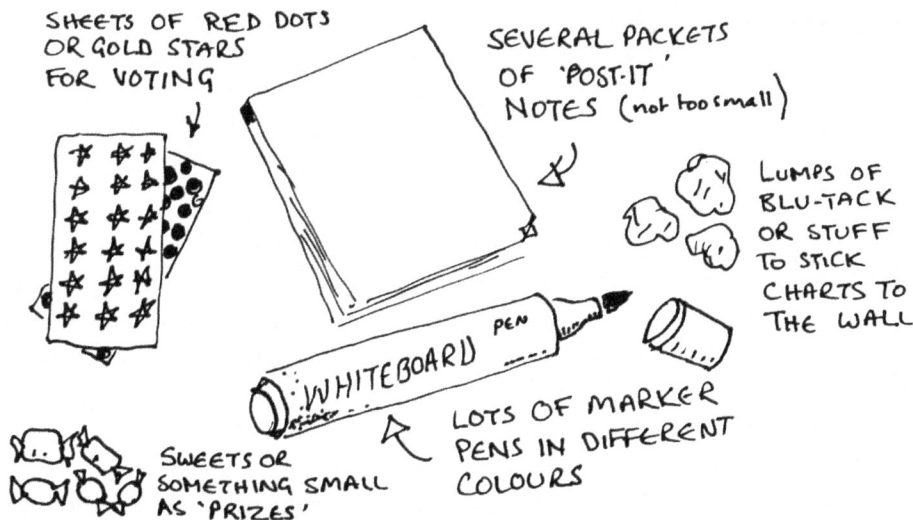

CASE STUDIES

Most of these activities work best when discussing a real site such as a museum, or real heritage issue. However, if you are using these activities to teach generic heritage skills, a case study of a heritage site or issue that is relevant to the group is useful. I use Robben Island Museum in South Africa as the basis for the activities to do with significance, as it covers a wide range of heritage issues. If preparing a case study, manage the amount of information you provide in accordance with the nature of the activity. I tend to use a few images and a map of the site and also provide some basic history. Too much information in a case study can be a distraction, although some activities do require more in-depth information, such as examples of reports.

FORMAL PRESENTATIONS

Most of these activities were originally developed because I found that written guidance or formal presentations were not an effective way of communicating the ideas and philosophy behind values-based thinking. That being said, if teaching or training, it can be useful to conclude a day with a formal presentation, just to reinforce the concepts that lie behind what might seem like a series of casual games or activities.

ROLE OF THE FACILITATOR

In facilitating activities, the critical thing is to observe group dynamics so as to find ways to bring people into the conversation and not impose your own views. Manage the energy of a group over a half-day or day workshop by using different types of activities with different learning styles. Structure each activity with a beginning, middle and end – introducing it, playing it and drawing out conclusions at the end. Don't let one activity run into another; mark the break between each firmly and clearly.

For each exercise, be clear about what is expected. Let people know how long they have, and always give people a warning before time is up. Stop an exercise as soon as the first person has finished so that you don't find yourself with bored participants.

Respect the knowledge and skills of people in the room, and use introductions to understand people's backgrounds and experience. For example, a group dealing with a church might include the vicar, the churchwarden, parishioners, an historian, an architectural specialist, the person who cuts the grass, a community group who use the hall, the Sunday school group etc.

Some facilitators like to use a short exercise at the start in order to set the ground rules for the day. Either you can suggest some or ask your audience to suggest them. This is important if you are working with a community group involved in a deeply contested heritage issue; otherwise I prefer to set such rules using activities that involve listening skills, making sure to respect and acknowledge different views in the room.

Icebreaker

The most common icebreaker I use is to ask everyone to introduce themselves and say what they have done previously. This provides a basis for demonstrating the range of different skills that apply to heritage management and also for including people in the discussion who may not have specialist heritage expertise. Anyone who has worked in retail, hospitality or cared for a family has important skills in relation to looking after heritage. Your role as workshop facilitator is to ensure that those voices are heard and not drowned out.

Encouraging and Capturing Feedback

If you have asked people to do something, provide adequate time for feedback and recognition of that effort. For each exercise, plan how you will do that. If you have a big group, for example, ask representatives of teams to give feedback or ask for selective feedback by theme.

A Bit of Theatre

Finally, use an element of theatre. Manage and maintain the energy in the room by using a variety of techniques, keeping things moving and ensuring that everyone can participate actively. If possible, add some drama through techniques such as:

- asking people to draw topics or objects from a hat – a lucky dip adds an element of genuine surprise
- using the clock or a timer to set strict deadlines for a bit of panic
- moving people around the room for different activities
- giving out small prizes such as sweets
- using drawings and pictures

Best of all, get out of the classroom so that your group can do or experience something – like seeing a museum from the perspective of a wheelchair user.

1

VALUING YOUR OWN HERITAGE

The activities in this section are simple ways to introduce a group to each other, drawing on issues such as identity, things that are important to them or things that they share in common such as places or other connections. They can be used at the beginning of any workshop or training day as a way to build connections within the group that will help the rest of the workshop run more smoothly.

Each activity introduces people to heritage by drawing on their own personal identity, history, memories and stories. Not only does this illustrate core concepts in heritage by exploring participants' own stories, but it also has relevance to the essential skills needed in heritage practice.

Thinking about the role of history and memory in shaping one's own life and sense of self is a very good foundation for then being able to work with, and indeed respect, the heritage of others. As cultural historian Professor Stuart Hall noted, heritage is a powerful mirror, and those who don't see themselves reflected in it are therefore excluded. A lack of respect for and understanding of individual identity, culture and history is often behind many of the problems people face – whether as an anonymous resident in a care home, or a young person feeling marginalized and excluded. Finding the words and images to capture – and share – that identity is an important starting point. Heritage practitioners need to be sensitive to and respect the heritage of others. These activities draw out some of the different factors that shape our identity – cultural factors, locational factors, family, spiritual values and others and the links between them. Finally, an activity relating to loss explores the impact of losing a place on one's own sense of self.

HERITAGE IS A POWERFUL
MIRROR - THOSE WHO DON'T
SEE THEMSELVES REFLECTED
IN IT ARE THEREFORE EXCLUDED

Stuart
Hall

❦ 1.1 INTRODUCTIONS – A SIMPLE QUIZ

This is a simple introductory activity for strangers or even colleagues who think they know each other. You can give it a bit more of a heritage flavour by asking people to focus on something that is part of their own heritage or history or culture. The activity is commonly used in any kind of training workshop to build connections between people.

⦂ *AIM*

To encourage people in the room to know each other better and be more confident about speaking out.

⦂ *PREPARATION*

Pens and paper, and perhaps a small prize for winners or winning teams.

⦂ *WHAT TO DO*

Ask everyone to:

> *Think of something that no one would know about you (and which you don't mind sharing).*
> *Write it down on a piece of paper but do not put your name on it.*

Gather all the pieces of paper together. Take the first one and write a number on it. Read out what it says; for example:

> *Number One: 'I hate cats'.*

Read out each of the other slips of paper, giving each a number, and ask people to write down their guess as to who it might be.

Try to keep the pieces of paper in order. Once you have read the whole list out, it is time to mark the answers. Ask each table to pass their guesses to the next table. Read out the slips in turn, and ask the originator to own up to their secrets. Who guessed correctly? How does knowing more about a person change your perception of them?

Guess who:
1. hates cats?
2. wanted to be an astronaut?
3. won a dancing competition?
4. was born in Tonga?
6. is really good at cryptic crosswords?

. . .

⚛ 1.2 PUT YOURSELF ON THE MAP – PLACE AND IDENTITY

This activity can either be used to introduce a group to each other or to explore the wider issue of place and identity. You could also use it as an introduction to a workshop on 'placemaking' in conjunction with some of the activities in section 4 or 6.

⦂ *AIM*

To encourage people to get to know each other and to understand their physical links to a particular place and each other.

⦂ *PREPARATION*

You need a bit of space to do this, so it works best if you are outside or have an area with no chairs. I learned this activity from my choir leader.

⦂ *WHAT TO DO*

Ask everyone to:

> *Imagine the floor is a map of the town or area. Please organize yourselves around the room according to where you live. Stand closest to the person who lives nearest to you.*

There will be a bit of chaos whilst people work themselves out. To make it easier, appoint one person to be, for example, London or the Town Hall and then tell people which way north is. If you have a very diverse group, allocate a continent to each corner of the room. People will need to work out who lives where and who their neighbours are. They can introduce themselves to the person (or people) who lives nearest to them.

⦂ *DISCUSSION*

If you are simply using this to introduce a group, there is no need for further discussion.

However, if you want to draw out the topic of how places are valued, open up a discussion on the link between place and identity. Ask the group:

- To what extent is your own identity shaped by the place where you live?
- How do connections to place shape your connections with others?
- Is identity relevant to thinking about the value of places?

🍇 1.3 MY HERITAGE, YOUR HERITAGE

Many heritage specialists use this activity or a variation on it. It doubles as both a way to introduce people to each other and a way to get people thinking about their own heritage and what is important about it.

⠿ *AIM*

To give each person a basic understanding of the value of cultural heritage and to make a link to their own personal heritage.

⠿ *PREPARATION*

In advance of the day, contact everyone who will be there to ask them to bring an object from home that has special meaning to them. Note that it does not have to be expensive or valuable – and they should not bring anything too precious or fragile.

⠿ *WHAT TO DO*

Depending upon numbers in the room, either go round the room and ask each person about the object they have brought with them and why it is important to them or, alternatively, ask each person to report back to their group table.

⠿ *DISCUSSION*

Ask people to think about the importance of personal heritage and the extent to which it resides in places or perhaps in less tangible things. You can also introduce the different kinds of significance that things might have; whilst everything in the exercise will have personal value, that value might also be aesthetic or social, or perhaps to do with belonging or connection. Think about how to capture those values in words or place them in categories.

THIS IS A BAG FOR CLOTHES PEGS. MY FATHER MADE IT FOR ME. I HAVE A NEW ONE, BUT I DON'T WANT TO THROW THIS OUT.

PEGS

❦ 1.4 WHO AM I? EXPLORING IDENTITY

Cultural heritage plays a powerful role in identity. Whilst biological descent may be one aspect of who we are, our culture, traditions and beliefs also shape the way that we see ourselves.

⠿ *AIM*

To contrast and compare different factors that shape our identity and to help foster an understanding of other people's identity.

⠿ *PREPARATION*

This is easiest to play in a room or open space with little furniture. Each person needs a pen and paper. You will need a board at the front to write on and coloured dots for voting.

⠿ *WHAT TO DO*

MY IDENTITY:

1. I live in Wales
2. My family come from India
3. I am a musician
4. I am a father
5. I love sailing

The factors might include place of birth or residence, school or college, religion, family, profession or skills, taste in music or sports team followed. Capture all the different factors that people have identified in a list on the board, leaving room for people to vote for what they consider to be the most influential.

Once the list is complete, give everyone five sticky dots to place next to the five factors on the list that have shaped them the most.

Ask people to start by working alone and ask the following:

Thinking about your own identity, please write down the five factors that have been most important to you in shaping your identity.

Identity factor	What is important to you
place you live	•
place of birth	• • •
school	•
Faith	• • • •
Skills	•
Job	• • •
taste in music	
Leisure activities	• • •
Ancestry + family	• • • • •
Friends	•

⠃⠄ *DISCUSSION*

Count up all the dots on the board. Identify the top five factors that the group values most. Compare this to the individual lists people had – are they the same or different? Does the list fall into different categories such as locational factors, cultural factors and biological factors?

⣏

VARIATION

This is an alternative version of 'Who Am I?'. It can be played if you have lots of space and want to keep people moving. Instead of the dot voting exercise, use the technique in 1.2: 'Put Yourself on the Map' to get people to map common identity factors.

⠃⠄ *What to Do*

Follow the instructions for 'Who am I?'. Pick one identity factor off the board; e.g. 'where I was born'. Ask one person to volunteer to stand in the middle of the room. Nominate one side of the room to be 'north'. Ask everyone else to:

> *Arrange yourselves in relation to how important this factor has been in shaping your identity, standing nearer to the person if it is important and further away if it isn't. Introduce yourselves to the people standing closest to you.*

If you have time, pick other identity factors from the list on the board, such as football or sports team followed. Again, ask people to introduce themselves to the person or people standing closest to them.

⠃⠄ *Discussion*

Discuss the different identity factors individuals decided to list in the first place. For example, if you chose 'where I was born' this is a geographical factor, whilst 'sports team followed' might be a cultural identity factor. Is there a degree of overlap between different identity factors?

Having introduced themselves to people who have assigned a similar amount of value to a given identity factor, how did the group feel? Did it change their attitude to other people in the room?

⬙ 1.5 WHY MY PLACE IS SPECIAL

This is a personal identity activity adapted for a particular place or area. Area or place could mean anything – a country, a state or county or even your neighbourhood. Adapt the exercise to the group you are working with.

⁞⁞ *AIM*

To think about the factors that shape the identity of places and what makes them special.

⁞⁞ *WHAT TO DO*

Get people to work in pairs. Ask them following:

> *Spend a couple of minutes thinking about your local area or neighbourhood.*
>
> *Explain to your partner how you feel about it and why it is special to you (or not).*
>
> *What makes it different from neighbouring places? Why do you care about it?*

Allow no more than 3 minutes for each participant, then call out 'change!'

⁞⁞ *DISCUSSION*

At the end of the exercise, ask each pair to draw up a list of the key factors that contribute to what makes a place special. The list may include some or all of the following:

- what happened there – history and archaeology
- built form
- people – the communities and individuals who have shaped the place
- landscape and topography
- spaces
- uses – what happens there?
- views and setting
- losses – what has disappeared?
- culture

Capture the key factors on a board at the front, and discuss the different ways in which we value places.

⁘ 1.6 OUR NEIGHBOURHOOD, OUR MAP

This is an activity for a group who all live in one area or neighbourhood. It would be useful at the start of a community consultation exercise about the future of a place or site.

⁘ *AIM*

To create a map of a place based on people's own memories and stories.

⁘ *WHAT TO DO*

Give each person five pieces of paper and ask them to:

> *Identify up to five landmarks in your neighbourhood and write the name of each landmark on a different piece of paper. For each landmark, draw it and write one thing about it, using one of the following headings:*

> *Hearsay*

> *Fact*

> *Personal connection*

> *History or tradition*

Those landmarks can be specific – such as a park bench – or general, such as a park. They don't necessarily need to be 'nice' things. For example, you might have a 'bleak car park' or an area of smelly drains.

Once that is complete, mark out the room or space you are in as north, south, east and west. Ask people to sticky-tape their pieces of paper on the floor in relation to each other to make a map of the local area. The result is a map of the whole area, based on how people perceive it.

⁘ *DISCUSSION*

You can now play with the map. Ask people to walk around it, putting ticks or crosses against those statements that they agree with. What are the shared perceptions? How do people's views differ? Is the way a local sees the neighbourhood different from the way a planner or heritage specialist might see it?

⚇ 1.7 THE MEANING OF LOST PLACES – EXPLORING THE POWER OF PLACE

This activity was inspired by a book that captures the stories of people who have lost places – to debt, road building, cyclones or migration (Read 1996). Each story is personal and emotional and reminds one of the power that places have over us and what they represent.

⠿ *AIM*

To help people understand the value of preservation by focusing on the impact of loss.

⠿ *WHAT TO DO*

Ask people to work in small teams. Ask one person from each team to:

Tell the rest of the team a story about a place that you have lost.

Ask the others to:

Gently draw out the impact of that on the life of the speaker and her/his family and friends.

Then ask people to:

Find a creative way to capture that impact (if not the details) in a way that can be shared.

It might be a drawing, a short poem or story, or a dramatic scene or mime. It should capture the essence of the loss and what it means, rather than the details.

⠿ *DISCUSSION*

Conclude with a wider discussion about loss of places, things or culture, what it means and how it impacts on people. What lessons does this have for heritage practice?

TELEPHONE BURNT IN THE BUSHFIRE

CANBERRA MUSEUM + ART GALLERY, 2013

2

ᐧᐧᐧᐧ

ENCOUNTERS WITH THE PAST

These activities challenge people to think about the different responses we have to encounters with the past. An encounter with the past is any way in which someone deliberately or accidentally comes into contact with something old. It might be a visit to a heritage asset such as a park, museum or site, packing up a family home or discovering something about one's own history.

Those encounters are an important starting point for understanding different heritage values. People who volunteer for or work in museums and heritage often assume that what visitors take away from a museum site or special place is a lesson in history. In practice, this is rarely the case – the response to visiting an old place is often deeply personal. People make connections with their own stories, or make links to knowledge they already have.

Encounters with the past can also be emotional – people may experience joy, sadness, peace, relaxation and many other feelings. Those emotions can be quite powerful and often shape our memories and feelings about a place.

The activities in this section are designed to help put into words some of what we learn when we encounter heritage and the accompanying feelings about it. They introduce basic ideas about experiences, learning and value.

⬞ 2.1 AN ENCOUNTER WITH THE PAST – LEARNING AND FEELING

This is the activity I use most to demonstrate the importance of emotions in thinking about the value of heritage. It is a good icebreaker at the beginning of a longer workshop on almost any practical heritage issue, such as planning, decision-making, access or interpretation. Although it is superficially simple, it can be used to draw out complex ideas around heritage learning, emotional responses to heritage and individual heritage.

It is structured in such a way as to also encourage participants to develop listening and storytelling skills – critical elements of heritage practice.

AIM

To demonstrate that what we learn from the past may not only be about history, and that encounters with heritage may have a strong emotional impact.

PREPARATION

Post-it notes, a whiteboard and a thickish pen to write with.

WHAT TO DO

Ask everyone in the room:

> *Think about a recent encounter you have had with heritage – ideally in the last day or so. How did it make you feel? What did you learn?*

Prompt them to think broadly about heritage – it does not have to be a heritage site but could be a family photograph, or a trip to the seaside, or walking past something old in the street. Next, ask people to work in pairs. Suggest the following:

> *Tell the person sitting next to you about your encounter with heritage. Tell them how it made you feel and then tell them what you learned.*

When they are done, ask each person in turn to report back their neighbour's encounter. If you have a very big group, just ask a selection of people.

MEGAN WAS WALKING PAST THE SITE OF HER OLD FAMILY HOME. IT MADE HER FEEL SAD. SHE LEARNED THAT A LOT OF HOUSES ARE BEING DEMOLISHED

⠿ *DISCUSSION*

As the group reports back, pick up on the points that relate to learning and the points that relate to feelings and write them on the whiteboard. Organize the emotions on one side of the board and learning points on the other. The two lists will raise lots of issues around the way we traditionally look at heritage and learning. For example, do we just learn about history from heritage encounters or are there other experiences we learn from? Explore the range of emotions that are on the board and ask whether these are actually ways in which heritage might be of value to people. Ask how it feels to have someone else tell your story, and perhaps use this to talk about the importance of listening and storytelling in heritage practice.

WHAT DID YOU LEARN ABOUT?

town planning

family

gardening

physics

my best friend

politics

HOW DID YOU FEEL?

SAD

INSPIRED

AWED

CONFUSED

GRUMPY

AT PEACE

⚛ 2.2 HISTORY LUCKY DIP – THE MEANING OF OBJECTS

This activity involves thinking about what an object might mean to someone. It is a good way of giving people confidence in dealing with unfamiliar objects or heritage issues. It is similar to 'My Heritage, Your Heritage' in the first section but less personalized.

⠿ *AIM*

To demonstrate the basic process of understanding and valuing a heritage object, and to give people the confidence to see that it is quite a simple thing to do!

⠿ *PREPARATION*

Flip chart, paper and pens. Opaque envelopes or bags (we used to use the zip-up folders you sometimes get at conferences), each with an item in it. The items should be anything that could be classed as heritage, such as:

- a chunk of old brick or a potsherd

- an old photograph

- a piece of lace or interesting fabric

- a fragment of manuscript

- a pine cone

- a teaspoon

an oar lock from a boat

a wooden elephant

a photograph

a key

a ring

Anything that is not too valuable and not too big but that has an obvious story can be used. The best objects are those that challenge assumptions – a photograph of a British Sikh soldier during the Second World War works well. If you are using an archaeological artefact such as a potsherd, you may need to help the group a little.

⠿ *WHAT TO DO*

Ask people to get into teams and have someone from each group pick an envelope at random. Tell them to put the item at the centre of a large piece of paper and create a spider diagram around it, setting out some of the reasons why it might be important. You may need to prompt teams to think about how the object might be important. You might demonstrate with one object yourself at the beginning.

⠗ *DISCUSSION*

Once they are done, ask one person from each team to report back, perhaps with someone else holding up the sheet of paper. Use the discussion to draw out bigger points about heritage and what it means. Touch on the different kinds of things you can learn and also underline the point that there are lots of different perspectives on heritage.

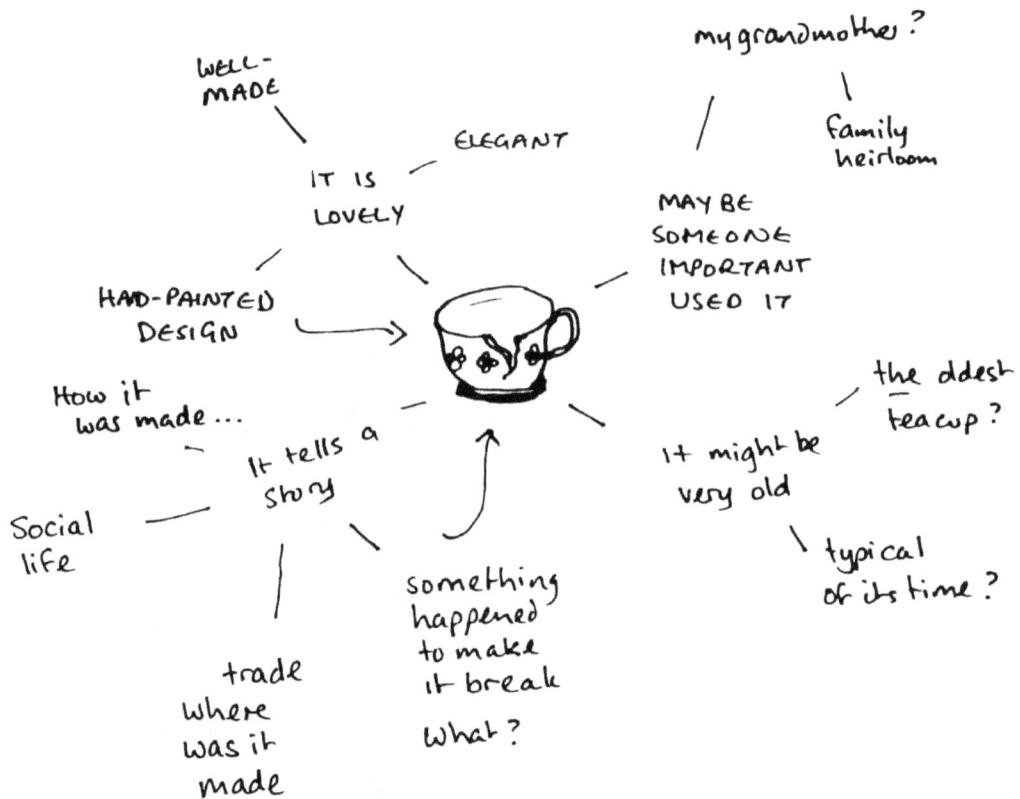

WELL-
MADE

ELEGANT

my grandmother?

family
heirloom

IT IS
LOVELY

MAY BE
SOMEONE
IMPORTANT
USED IT

HAND-PAINTED
DESIGN

the oldest
teacup?

How it
was made...

It tells a
story

It might be
very old

typical
of its time?

Social
life

trade
where
was it
made

something
happened
to make
it break

What?

⚘ 2.3 LEARNING TO LISTEN

One of the skills that is critical to heritage practice is the ability to ask questions and, more importantly, to listen to the answers. Ironically, this can be most difficult for those with a strong specialist background, for example in ecology, history or archaeology, where that knowledge can make it harder to be open to different perspectives on the value of a place or heritage item. That being said, the intention is not to devalue the research skills that underpin the different heritage disciplines.

⠞ *AIM*

To increase skills in thinking about the value of heritage by learning to ask questions and listen to answers.

⠞ *WHAT TO DO*

Put people into teams of about four or five. Ask each team to nominate a 'Heritage Expert' – someone in the team who knows a place, an object or a collection ('the asset') well and cares about it deeply. Explain that it can be something that is important to them as an individual – it does not have to be a formal heritage site. However, it does need to be something that they are comfortable talking about and sharing with others.

Ask each team to nominate a 'Writer' to capture information on a sheet of paper and a 'Speaker' to feed back to everyone at the end. You (the facilitator) are going to be the Judge. Read out the following task:

> *The Expert has one minute to describe the asset to the rest of the group. The rest of you may*
> *then pose questions to the expert in order to deduce the value of the asset.*

Give people 10 minutes to complete the task, then go around the room and ask each Speaker to tell the group about the heritage item and explain why it is important to the Expert. The winning team is the one whose Speaker can persuade the Judge that 'their' heritage asset is the most important.

⠞ *DISCUSSION*

If you have a confident group, ask the Experts whether they feel that the essence of the place or object was captured by the rest of the team or not.

⚘

VARIATION

To make it more difficult, add an extra rule: the Expert can only answer 'yes' or 'no' to each question from their team. In this case, you may need to allow more time.

❦ 2.4 PROFESSOR OF ARCHAEOLOGY

This introduces the idea that there are multiple ways to interpret a single object – something that can apply to all sorts of different heritage assets.

⁘ *AIM*

To remind people that one object can have multiple stories.

⁘ *PREPARATION*

You will need to bring an object. It does not have to be old; it might be a rolled up newspaper or a pen – in fact, the more ordinary the better.

⁘ *WHAT TO DO*

Ask everyone to sit in a circle. Explain that this object was excavated from an archaeological site. The site has been long forgotten, and no one is quite sure what the object is any more:

> *Each of you has been appointed to the post of professor of archaeology. You have come to-gether at a conference to debate the purpose of this mysterious object. The first person in the circle will tell everybody what the function, history and value of the object is, before handing it to the next person. Their job is to disagree politely with the previous professor and provide a very different interpretation of its function, history and value. And so on round the circle.*

⁘ *DISCUSSION*

How far did the activity go? How many different interpretations of one object did the group find? What were the different kinds of values that emerged in the process?

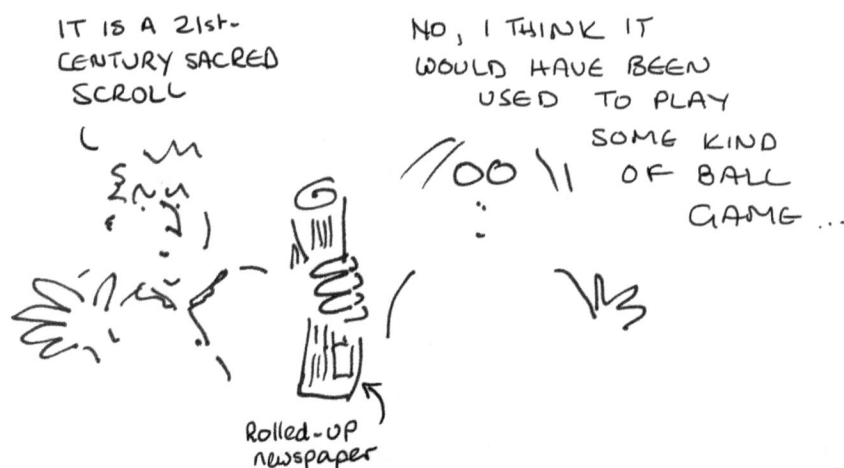

IT IS A 21st-
CENTURY SACRED
SCROLL

NO, I THINK IT
WOULD HAVE BEEN
USED TO PLAY
SOME KIND
OF BALL
GAME ...

Rolled-UP
newspaper

✿ 2.5 THE DEAD MARKER PEN – INTRODUCING HERITAGE VALUES

This activity is part of 3.3 but can also be used on its own as a quick introduction to heritage values. It does not have to involve a marker pen – I have also used my shoe (even better if it is a bit worn), a bit of house brick or a coffee cup. Ideally – and it's more fun and dramatic – pick an object at random in the room.

⁞⁞· AIM

To demonstrate that what makes something part of our heritage is not what it is in itself (e.g. the fact that it is an object or a building) but the value we place on it.

THIS PEN DOES NOT WORK ANY MORE – WHAT MIGHT STOP ME FROM THROWING IT AWAY?

⁞⁞· PREPARATION

You'll need a flip chart or board, pens and an object (in this case a marker pen).

⁞⁞· WHAT TO DO

Ask the group:

Imagine that this pen no longer works. What would prevent me from throwing it into the bin?

People will begin to throw in ideas, such as, 'it may have been used by an important person'. As each idea comes from the floor, note it on the flip chart.

Part way through, ask if anything can be learned from the pen. You are looking for what are in effect 'evidential' values. For a pen, these might be the design, manufacture, ideas about recycling, ideas about technology (especially if you are using an old style flip chart), information about communication and learning styles. Ask what the pen might suggest about the room you're in if it was dug up by a future archaeologist.

VALUES

old   beautiful   an important person
associated with   an important event
typical   the best
the last   designed by someone famous   valuable materials
re-useable
Your grandmother gave it to you
trade
materials   purchasing
design   the economy
manufacturing
Ink   writing
it tells a story   communication
who used it   about this place – how the room was used   technology   innovation

⁞⁞· DISCUSSION

The group will soon pick up on the fact that you are identifying a range of heritage values for an object, building or place. Keep going till you have a good range of values captured on the flip chart.

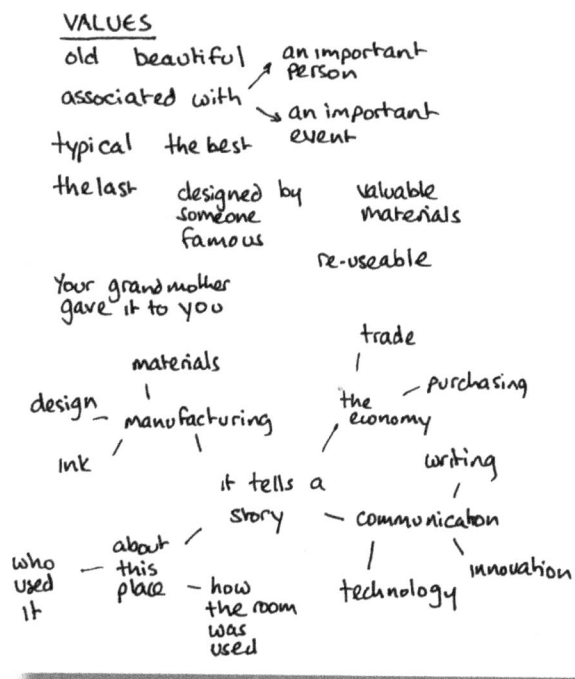

3

VALUES IN CONSERVATION PLANNING –
THE BIG PICTURE

The activities in this section go together to illustrate the core set of ideas that underpin the rest of this book. They work through five steps that enable people to understand the different ways in which an object, collection or place might be of value and show how understanding that value can be used to sustain or manage it. The five steps are:

1. What have we got? (understanding)
2. Why does it matter? (heritage value)
3. What is happening to it? (vulnerability)
4. What needs to be done about it? (management or sustainability)
5. Who needs to be involved? (stakeholders)

Taken together, these five steps are a useful way of thinking about almost any heritage issue. They also provide the structure for a more formal written values-based conservation management plan.

Like other activities in this book, they can be used to 'do' or to 'teach'. They could be used as part of a community engagement process in order to understand how people value a specific place or site, as the starting point for a wider exercise on place-making or a new design, or alternatively to teach to a group of students or trainees the basic principles of how values shape the way we practice heritage.

In the context of a community engagement exercise, these activities provide a logical framework through which to draw out the knowledge and views of everyone in a group. Once that information has been captured, it can be used where it is critical to include community views, such as in managing a heritage site or drafting a formal written plan. In the latter case, there will need to be a note-taker and a proper record of the day. It may also be important to ensure that you have the agreement of participants to make or keep that record.

Where the exercises are being used generically to teach the basic concept of 'values-based practice' in heritage, the facilitator can either use a case study or draw on participants' own knowledge to illustrate the key steps in the process.

⚇ 3.1 STARTER – PERCEPTIONS OF CONSERVATION AND HERITAGE

This initial activity is to get people thinking and sets the scene for the rest of the activities in this section.

⚇ AIM

To think about what 'conservation' and 'heritage' mean, and to acknowledge that there can be both positive and negative views.

⚇ PREPARATION

For all the activities in this section, you will need a flip chart with plenty of paper and thick marker pens in various colours. Note that a whiteboard is not ideal, as the activity requires the sheets of paper to be torn off and held up and/or tacked to the wall.

⚇ WHAT TO DO

The aim is to get everyone talking about heritage in a very broad sense. Ask:

> *What do the words 'conservation', 'preservation' or 'heritage' mean to you?*

If you are working with a heritage organization, ask if they have a specific definition of 'heritage', 'conservation' or 'preservation'.

If you have a variety of heritage professions in the room, you might ask about the ways in which words like preservation or conservation are used. The meanings of words can also vary between countries – 'preservation' in the US and 'conservation' in the UK.

As the discussion goes on, tease out negative as well as positive views (such as 'heritage stops progress'). Capture the points on a flip chart – put positive views in one colour and negative views in another colour.

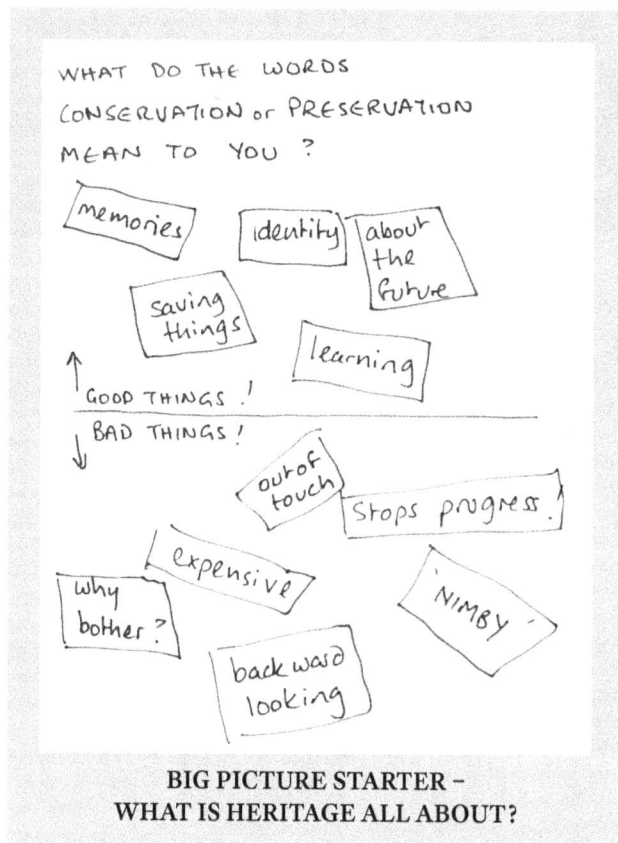

**BIG PICTURE STARTER –
WHAT IS HERITAGE ALL ABOUT?**

⠃⠃· *DISCUSSION*

In discussion, compare and contrast the different views of heritage. Do the views of people who care about heritage or are involved in conserving or preserving it match the views of those who are not directly involved in caring for heritage, such as people in the media or politicians? If not, why not? Are there different perceptions of the value of heritage?

⸬ 3.2 WHAT HAVE YOU GOT? UNDERSTAND WHAT IS THERE NOW

This covers the first step in cultural heritage practice – being able to describe or tell the story of a collection, place or thing (or intangible heritage asset). It shows how almost any heritage asset is made up of different heritage elements.

⸬ *AIM*

To understand a particular heritage asset (or 'heritage' in general) as the first step in caring for it, and to demonstrate that most heritage assets are made up of more than one kind of heritage.

⸬ *WHAT TO DO*

Explain:

> *For this activity, I will pick an asset. I want you to list the different elements that are part of it.*

To help the group get going, start by identifying one or two elements yourself. For a museum, you might start with 'the collection' or 'the building' it is in, for a park, 'the trees' or 'the views'. Write the elements on the flip chart. Check that the group is thinking broadly about different elements that make up a heritage site or asset. For example, if you are dealing with an industrial asset such as a preserved railway, ask if there is any biodiversity along the line. For a museum collection, ask if there are documents, related items in other collections or oral histories associated with the collections. Aim for at least twenty different elements.

HERITAGE
buildings   landscapes faith
Collections   memories species
trains   bridges   music
interiors   memory   furniture
art   dance   archives   biodiversity
industrial remains   archaeology
skills   stories   war memorials
language   habitats   traditions
myths and legends

BIG PICTURE STEP ONE – UNDERSTANDING HERITAGE

⸬ *DISCUSSION*

Use the list or elements on the flip chart to discuss the nature of heritage places, objects or collections and introduce some basic concepts in heritage practice. For example:

• **Tangible and intangible heritage.** Review the list to see whether both tangible and intangible kinds of heritage have been identified. Perhaps circle the intangibles in a different colour. Discuss the way heritage assets embrace both. Explore whether the group identified more tangible or intangible heritage, and if there is more intangible heritage (there often is), think about whether that balance is reflected in heritage practice.

- **Other stories.** Unless we stop and look for the different elements that make up a heritage asset, we can miss the many different stories that form part of that heritage. And the stories we miss are the ones that we don't respect, and as a result, may inadvertently destroy.

- **Heritage specialisms.** Discuss which professions/specialists deal with which kind of heritage – e.g. buildings (architects, surveyors), collections (conservators, curators), archaeology (traditional owners, archaeologists), oral history (oral historians), etc. Explore the fact that one heritage site or asset may include different heritage elements, and thus various specialisms need to work together. Don't exclude volunteers from this discussion – often volunteers will bring their own specialist knowledge of one area of heritage to a project.

- **Specialist biases.** Look at the list and spot any information gaps. Most groups are quick to identify the heritage elements that they know about but need to be prompted to identify those they are less familiar with. For example, a group who works with buildings may be slow to identify any natural heritage at a site (and vice versa). Use this to show how we often focus on looking after the heritage we know best and pay less attention to the heritage that is not our area of expertise.

Like the other steps in 'The Big Picture' this is a brief introduction to a far more complex process. The point of 'The Big Picture' is to show how each of the steps are linked, so you may need to move on quickly. But because it raises so many issues, you can always come back to this list and explore it in more detail later on, for example after 4.4: 'Understanding a Heritage Asset – Phasing'.

❦ 3.3 WHY DOES IT MATTER?

The next step in the process is at the heart of values-based practice. It introduces the big ideas about heritage values as the basis for moving on to the third step – understanding how values influence what we do.

I introduce this step by using 'The Dead Marker Pen' (2.5) to create a dramatic transition from understanding a heritage asset to articulating its value. This activity also demonstrates that the values that apply to one kind of heritage asset can also apply to others. I then move straight into exploring all of the different values for the heritage. Instead of a marker pen you can use another random object in the room, such as your shoe or a coffee mug.

⠿ *AIM*

To show that what makes something worth keeping is not the fact that it is an object, building or species (or traditions or knowledge or language) but the *value* that people place on it.

⠿ *WHAT TO DO*

Suggest the following:

> *Let's review the information written down on the first flip chart. Does it suggest that everything is heritage? And is this coffee mug (or pen or shoe) that I present to you part of heritage too?*

Spend a moment encouraging a debate over whether a coffee mug can be a heritage item or not. Then ask:

> *If this coffee mug was broken (or shoe was worn out or pen stopped working), what might prevent you from throwing it away?*

You are looking to capture different reasons to keep the coffee cup/shoe/pen. It might be the first or the last such coffee cup/shoe/pen; it might be typical; it might have been used by a famous person. It could have been repaired or repurposed. Capture all these points on a new sheet of paper. The group will soon realize that you are talking about the different values for heritage.

Next, return to the bigger issue of the site/collection or heritage in general. Ask:

> *Do all of the values that apply to the coffee cup apply as easily to the site/collection/heritage in general? If so, are there other values that the asset might have in addition to the ones we have discussed so far?*

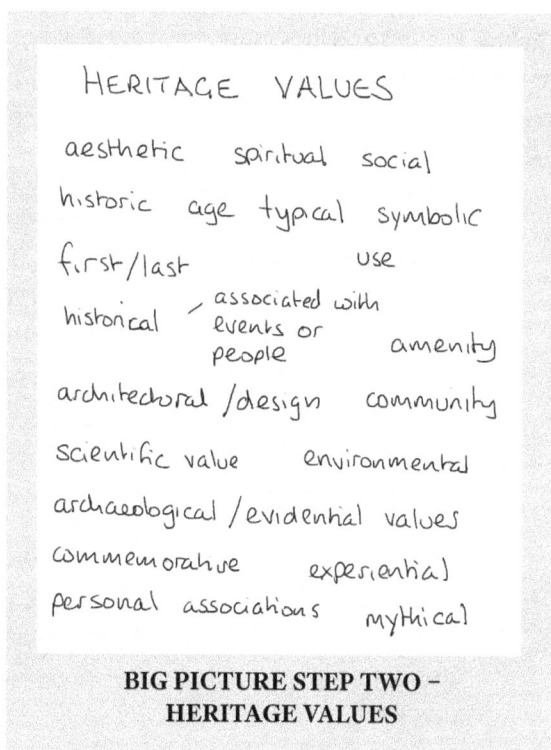

HERITAGE VALUES

aesthetic   spiritual   social

historic   age   typical   symbolic

first/last   use

historical   / associated with
                events or
                people   amenity

architectural /design   community

scientific value   environmental

archaeological /evidential values

commemorative   experiential

personal associations   mythical

**BIG PICTURE STEP TWO –
HERITAGE VALUES**

Widen the discussion to identify the different kinds of reasons that people might value the asset. You are looking for a chart full of words such as *beautiful, rare, designed by well-known architect, peaceful, associated with an event or people that are important in their own right,* as well as emotional responses, personal connections, amenity, and spiritual and practical values like utility.

DISCUSSION

Prompt the group to think widely by asking questions such as:

- Does everything that matters have to be rare? Is there any value in something that is typical?
- Do things have to be old to be valuable?
- Are there emotional connections?
- Are the values associated with heritage always pleasant or comfortable?

If working on a specific heritage site, discuss whether there are any difficult memories or events associated with the site. Explore whether it matters to keep places or things that have problematic or difficult connotations. If this activity relates to heritage in general, ask the group to give an example of a difficult place or thing that we might want to keep, and then think about why we would keep it.

Conclude the discussion with the core concept that what makes something part of the heritage is not that it is a building, or an object, or a place or intangible asset, but the value that we place on it. To illustrate this, compare and contrast this flip chart with the previous one.

Further Discussion

Heritage values and how they are defined is a huge and complex subject, and many of the other activities in Chapter 4 explore these ideas in more depth. If there is discussion time I often introduce two other key concepts regarding heritage values – the difference between values and significance and the idea that values change.

Degrees of significance. With the group, tease out the different levels or degrees of significance that lie behind, for example, World Heritage Sites, nationally protected buildings or sites of local importance. For museum collections, ask if objects have different levels or degrees of value – are some more important than others? If dealing with biodiversity, ask whether some habitats or species are more important than others, and if so, how is that importance or significance defined?

How values change. It is likely that someone will have already identified the fact that values change as part of the previous discussion. Use this activity to drill down into this issue further, or if time is short, do it at another time as a separate activity (see also 4.1).

THRESHOLDS FOR SIGNIFICANCE

international
national
state
regional
local
personal

more protection

Introduce this topic by surveying the range of different heritage values on the page, and then ask:

> *Are these values fixed or do they vary? And if so, how might they vary?*

Discuss the different factors that can cause our perceptions of value to change. These will include time, knowledge, your own culture and identity, political context, experiences, fashion and many others. Ask whether future generations might have different perceptions of value to our own? I talk about how ideas about value are central to heritage, but at the same time, values are complex, can be expressed in different ways and inevitably change through time. It is what makes heritage fascinating, but also complex and sensitive.

HOW DO VALUES VARY?

time

Social Contexts

Knowledge

events

Scarcity

beliefs

economic context

❦ 3.4 WHAT IS HAPPENING TO IT?

An important step in this process is to understand how and in what way the significance or value of something might be at risk. Without understanding that, it is very difficult to then go on to think about how best to care for it.

⦂⦂ *AIM*

To identify the different things that might put a heritage asset at risk.

⦂⦂ *PREPARATION*

Use a new sheet of paper.

⦂⦂ *WHAT TO DO*

Ask:

> *What are all the things that might damage or destroy the site/collection/object?*

The group may begin with issues such as major incidents or disasters. Write them down but then go on to prompt for things relating to site management, such as: *lack of maintenance, no opportunities for people to get involved, poor management, lack of research etc.*

Discuss whether heritage can be damaged by new development. What about compliance with legislation or regulations – such as environmental or health regulations or requirements for disability access? Is there potential for heritage specialists to do damage? Might visitors damage places? Write the risks that have been identified on the chart. I don't prompt discussion at this stage, but rather move quickly on to the next step.

WHAT MIGHT DAMAGE THIS
OBJECT / PLACE / BUILDING ?

lack of maintenance

poor repairs / disasters
  conservation

visitors !   climate   poor
             change   development

lack of   complying with - health
skills   legislation eg   +
                               safety

experts !!   lack of   ? too much
              money   money

lack of   people   poor marketing
security

climate   poor
change   management   ...etc.

**BIG PICTURE STEP THREE –
DAMAGE (RISKS)**

♨ 3.5 WHAT DO WE NEED TO DO ABOUT IT?

This step moves from the narrow view of conservation as being just about repairing things to a wider view of conservation as sustainability. It reminds people that managing heritage is as much about managing people as it is about managing physical things.

⠿ *AIM*

The aim of this step is to focus on what is involved in managing or caring for a particular site/collection/object/place/intangible asset (or for students – heritage in general).

⠿ *PREPARATION*

Start a new sheet of paper.

⠿ *WHAT TO DO*

Ask:

> *What do we need to do to ensure that this site/collection (or the heritage) will still be here in fifty years' time?*

To get started, write down something easy on the flip chart – e.g. *repair the buildings*. Work up to a sheet full of words that should include all of the activities that a heritage manager might deal with. Once again, capture as many as possible in order to demonstrate that heritage practice (in the sense of sustaining a site, place, collection or intangible asset in the long term) is a complex activity that goes well beyond physical work and finding resources. It also includes working with people, research and understanding, interpretation and storytelling, as well as events, engaging with media, commercial enterprises, etc.

You may need to prompt for a few controversial things – ask, for example:

> *Does developing new facilities or finding new uses for a heritage asset help ensure its survival?*

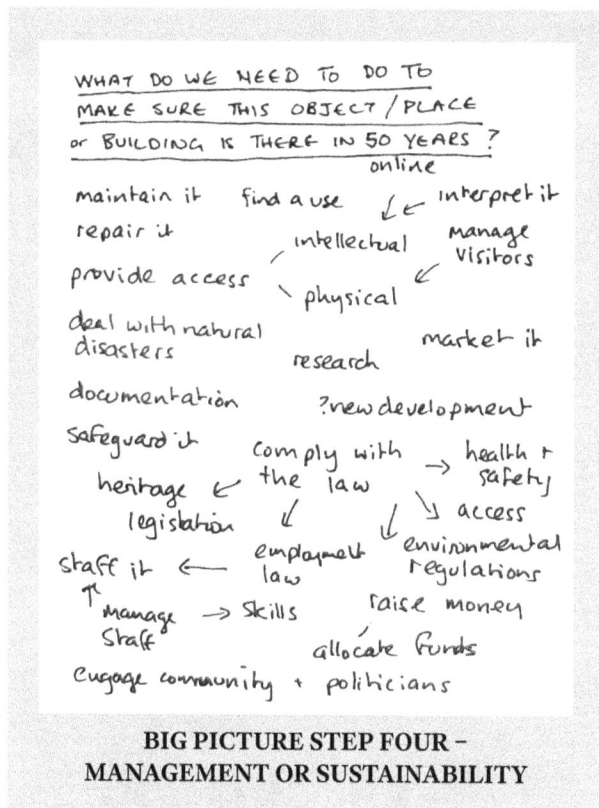

WHAT DO WE NEED TO DO TO
MAKE SURE THIS OBJECT / PLACE
or BUILDING IS THERE IN 50 YEARS?
online
maintain it   find a use   interpret it
repair it   intellectual   manage visitors
provide access   physical
deal with natural disasters   market it
                 research
documentation   ?new development
safeguard it   comply with   health + safety
heritage   the law   access
legislation   environmental regulations
staff it   employment law
manage staff → Skills   raise money
                 allocate funds
engage community + politicians

BIG PICTURE STEP FOUR – MANAGEMENT OR SUSTAINABILITY

The issue of money will probably come up. Probe it – ask what happens if you do not get funding and, indeed, if you do get funding. Ask about staffing, the importance of finding the right skills and the other things that need to happen as part of daily site management. If it does not come up spontaneously, suggest that the group think about the importance of using heritage sites (or languages, collections and skills) and whether that helps to sustain them.

At the end, label the sheet of paper 'Management or sustainability'.

⠿ 3.5.1 BRINGING IT ALL TOGETHER – THE REVEAL!

You are now going to use the four main sheets of paper to illustrate the four steps in values-based practice. Tear off the step three 'Damage (risks)' sheet and hold it up beside the 'Management' chart. Are there any similarities between these two sheets? Usually there will be some common issues; for example, visitors, changes or complying with regulations might figure on both charts. This clearly demonstrates that everything that you need to do to manage (or sustain) an asset also has the capacity to damage it or make it vulnerable. This is a key point to emphasize. Having established that everything you need to do to manage (or sustain) heritage also has the potential to damage it, there is now a conundrum!

Next, tear off the other two sheets – step one 'heritage' and step two 'values'. Select volunteers to hold up each of the four pieces of paper and organize them so they are standing in a line in order of the basic steps of the exercise. Talk about the four steps. Show how each step in the process is related and that you can't do one without the other. Explain that values are critical to management. Note that many planners start with step four – their management aims and objectives, rather than step one (understanding the complexity of what is there now) and step two (why it matters), before thinking about what needs to happen. This top-down approach has the potential to create problems for communities and for heritage managers. Show that the four steps provide a simple way of approaching complex issues.

If you are going on to do further activities using these charts, stick them up on the wall or on a board.

⚛ 3.6 . . . AND WHO NEEDS TO BE INVOLVED?

The final step is to help the group understand the need to involve people in managing or sustaining heritage.

⁞⁚ *AIM*

To introduce the importance of stakeholders.

⁞⁚ *PREPARATION*

Use a new sheet of paper. You will need to draw a picture of a bad fairy on it, so you may need to practise in advance of the workshop (or use mine).

⁞⁚ *WHAT TO DO*

As you draw the picture, tell the following story to the group:

> *When the baby princess was being christened, her mother the queen invited the good fairies to the christening but forgot to invite the bad fairy. Of course it was the bad fairy who later created problems for the princess.*

Discuss whether there are 'bad fairies' associated with heritage projects, sites or organizations and, if so, name them. Using a new piece of paper, write down the names people give you – usually you will get things like *local communities, funders, the media, grumpy neighbours*.

If the list is a bit thin, ask whether scientists, curators, archaeologists or historians can be bad fairies? If you are a manager or representing an organization, ask if you yourself have bad fairy potential?

The drawing illustrates the critical point of stakeholder engagement – that any of us have the potential to be 'bad fairies' if we are not involved in important decisions at the right time and in the right way. At the end write 'Stakeholders' at the top of the chart.

⁞⁚ *DISCUSSION*

Conclude the five steps by explaining that the group have just been through the values-based planning process. If they have done this exercise for a specific asset, they should now have a very good sense of the key issues in terms of understanding, managing and valuing an asset and recognizing who needs to be involved.

⚜ 3.7 YOUR VISION FOR HERITAGE – THE MISSING STEP

One of the most commonly asked questions is where and how does the process of establishing a vision for the future of a heritage asset come into the values-based planning process (for example, you might want to imagine a new visitor centre or an immersive new visitor experience), but the answer is it doesn't.

Designing a new concept vision is typically a top-down process that starts with an idea or a solution. It often means making assumptions about what is important to people.

Values-based thinking is the opposite – it starts with what is there, why it matters and to whom and uses that as a springboard for thinking about how to pass it on to future generations. The new visitor centre might be one way of doing that, but it may not be the only way.

Values-based planning is humble; it assumes you don't have all the answers and that in order to find them out you need to listen and learn for solutions to emerge. It subverts the 'power-based' model of heritage management or design that imposes solutions and then fits them to the place or the site. It is slow, not always easy and involves dealing with conflicting values. It requires skills in listening and the ability to articulate rather than impose ideas of value. It involves creativity in drawing ideas out of other people.

Having worked with the right group of people to understand what is there, why it matters, what some of the risks are and what things might need to be done to create 'future heritage', the floor is now set for shaping a vision, if that is what you need to do. But be aware that making it happen will involve engaging with all of the things that have emerged through the values-based process.

4

EXPLORING VALUE AND SIGNIFICANCE IN MORE DEPTH

This section contains activities that explore the concept of values and significance in more detail. They are especially designed for people who manage or make decisions about cultural heritage places such as historic buildings, landscapes, monuments, memorials, or areas such as towns, where the way that significance is articulated has a huge influence on how the place will be managed or protected. The activities could also be adapted for museum collections, especially where there is a need to define a collection of national importance or create meta-data for collections.

As the previous activities showed, every heritage decision involves a conscious or unconscious assessment of value and significance. When you protect a site, manage something, talk to a community group, develop a plan, or repair a roof, your approach will be shaped by your understanding of what matters and why.

But putting value and significance into words is a core heritage skill that must be learned and requires practice. It involves listening to different voices, processing a lot of research, finding stories in a mass of information, and being aware of different specialist disciplines. It involves ethics, respect for different views, an awareness of your own cultural biases, and, above all, the ability to capture complex ideas well.

Too often, the way that cultural heritage is regulated or managed results in people trying to force ideas about meaning into rigid boxes. This is because in order for a heritage asset to be formally protected it is necessary to demonstrate that it meets both the type of value that is protected and also the right level or degree of significance. The intention is usually to make a robust recommendation that can't be challenged legally, but the effect is often to narrow down protection to one or two aspects of a place. For example, a building might be protected for its nationally important architectural qualities but not for its locally important qualities such as its use as a pub or school

One of the exercises in this section involves writing a formal statement of significance. The other exercises explore significance from different perspectives. I would not advise using these activities until after the group has done the activities in Section 3, 'The Big Picture', because they assume an understanding of, and familiarity with, the concepts that were introduced there.

🍇 4.1 STARTER – VALUES CHANGE...

Almost as soon as you write a statement of significance, it changes or is out of date. This is a little starter exercise for a longer workshop or full day focusing on significance.

⠿ *AIM*

To remind everyone that values change.

⠿ *WHAT TO DO*

Get everyone to work in small groups. Ask everyone to:

> *Think about something that you hated as a child and now like. Take it in turns to share with the other people in your group what it was and what factors caused you to change your mind.*

Use an example from your own life – for example, mine is sport.

For the next part:

> *Identify a heritage item, place or thing that you once thought was boring but now think is interesting. What caused the change of mind set?*

To use another example, I used to be uninterested in historic locomotives, but then I worked with people who were passionate about them and found myself looking at trains in a different way.

⠿ *DISCUSSION*

Have a quick discussion about the way in which values change and the factors that might cause them to change such as the passage of time; changing knowledge about a site; the understanding of different voices; the social, economic or political context; fashion or location. Then open up a discussion about how values might change in the future.

🍇

VARIATION

You could introduce the idea of the 'Thirty Year Rule'. A number of cultural heritage protection regimes have a rule that suggests you should not protect something for at least thirty years after it has been built, as it takes that long to establish whether and how it matters. Is this a good idea? What role does the passage of time have in changing perceptions of value?

⚶ 4.2 THE 'FRIED EGG' OF VALUE – THE DIFFERENCE BETWEEN DESIGNATION AND MANAGEMENT VALUES

This question always creates a lot of confusion and may very well arise during the discussion of values. I touch on it briefly as part of 'The Big Picture', but you may also want to do this activity in its own right or in conjunction with activities such as 'Statement of Significance – Designation' (4.8.1) and 'Statement of Significance – Management Plan' (4.8.2).

⠿ *HOW TO PREPARE*

Go back to the sheet of paper on which you recorded the range of values from the 'Big Picture Step Two' in Section 3. If it is not available, create a new list, perhaps using 'The Dead Marker Pen' (2.5).

⠿ *WHAT TO DO*

Look at the values on the sheet of paper and ask:

> *If you were going to designate/nominate a site on, for example, a national list, which of these values would/could you take into account?*

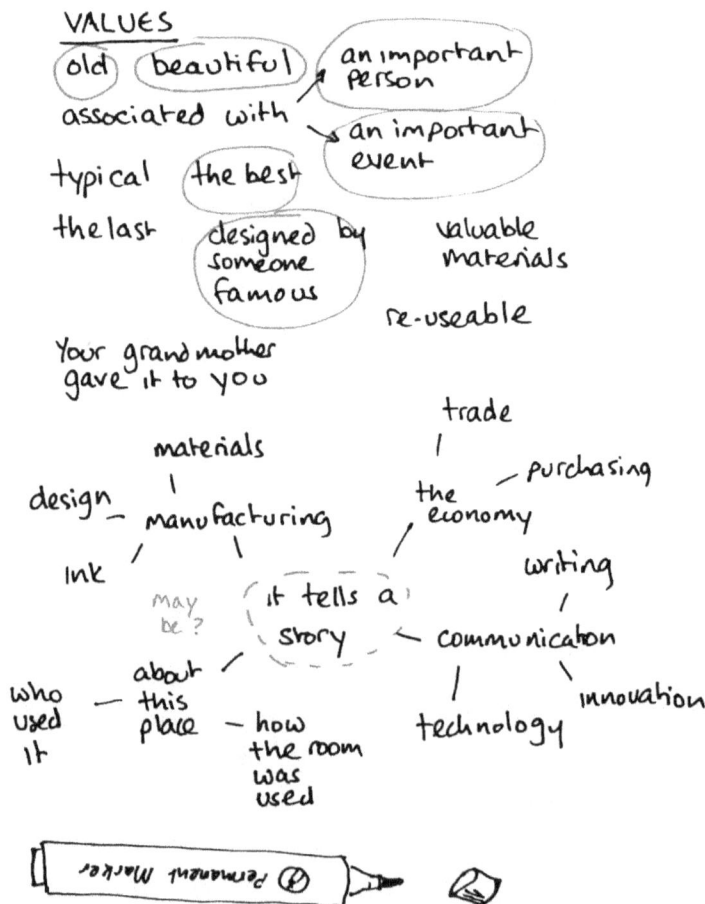

Using another colour, circle the ones the group selects. For example, for listed buildings in the UK, it may be the 'aesthetic value' or 'association with an individual' but not necessarily the personal value or the memories associated with something. For a species, it might be its 'rarity'.

Note that the narrow range of values that might be put on a list or register (e.g. aesthetic qualities) is not the whole story. This underlines the much bigger point that managing heritage sites often requires taking into account a far wider range of values than the relatively narrow range referred to in formal law or policy. I use the example of dog-walking in a park. A park may be protected for its natural heritage values, but people who want to walk their dogs there might assign greater value to its dog-friendliness. To illustrate this, I draw a fried egg – in the yolk are the values that are taken into account when protecting a place or item; on the egg white are the values that we need to take into account when we manage it.

THE FRIED EGG OF VALUE

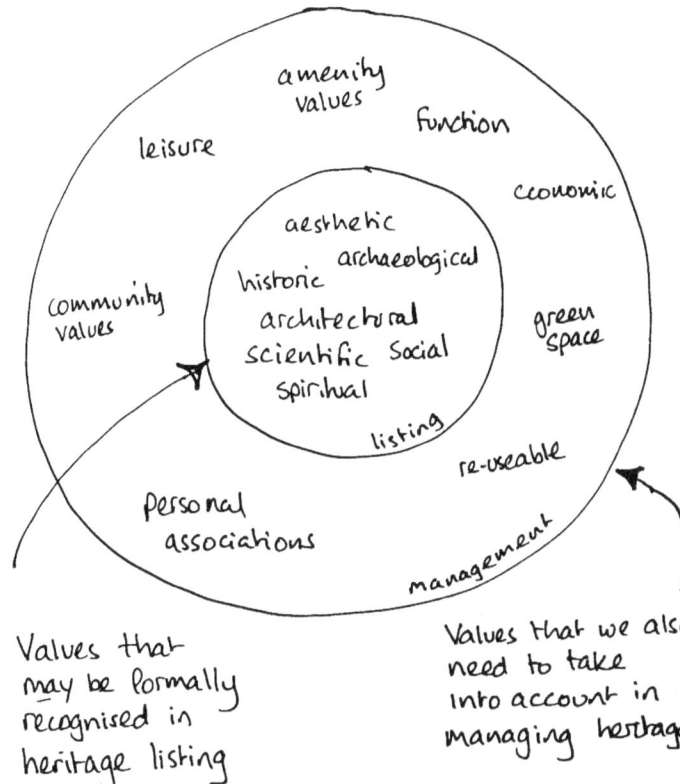

Use the fried egg to prompt a discussion about the different kinds of values. Only one set of values is likely to be mentioned in the designation document (e.g. the World Heritage Inscription). The result can be the exclusion of communities and/or a situation where one kind of heritage (e.g. natural heritage) is managed whilst other kinds (e.g. health benefits of outdoor exercise) are not.

⁘ 4.3 TIME, SPACE AND STAKEHOLDERS – THREE DIFFERENT APPROACHES TO HERITAGE VALUES

The whole issue of how best to articulate heritage value is complex. The approach most commonly used in heritage management is to explore different types of value (e.g. architectural, historical etc.). However, you can also look at value from different perspectives – such as through time, in space or from the point of view of different stakeholders. This activity explores those perspectives and is particularly useful for anyone who needs to write a statement of significance, a heritage impact assessment, risk assessment, conservation statement or management plan.

⁘ *AIM*

To illustrate three different approaches to articulating heritage values and explore the strengths and weaknesses of each.

⁘ *PREPARATION*

You will need the sheets of paper that you created as part of Section 3, 'The Big Picture', particularly the 'Heritage' and 'Values' charts. You may also need a laptop/projector/screen or copies if you plan to introduce a case study. Allow a good hour and a half or more for this – at least 20 minutes to do the activity and half an hour or more for feedback. If you are training or teaching heritage students, you will need to introduce a case study and provide some supporting material. I use Robben Island in South Africa as a case study. I put together a short presentation with key images and then talk through the main phases of the site, from earliest times to the present day. I give teams a photocopy of a map.

⁘ *WHAT TO DO*

Explain that:

> *Each team is going to prepare a statement of significance for this site using a different topic.*
> *At the end we will compare different approaches.*

Unless you are working with a place everyone knows well, present a case study. Assuming that the case study is a place, allocate a topic to each team (a maximum of five or six teams works best, otherwise feedback takes too long). The topics will depend upon the heritage asset but might include:

Team one – the built heritage

Team two – the landscape

Team three – the collections associated with the place

Team four – each phase through time

Team five – the perspective of one or more stakeholders

Ask each team to present their statement of significance, starting with the teams dealing with spatial topics (buildings/landscape and collections if included), then the team looking at significance through time and finally the team dealing with stakeholders.

DISCUSSION

Here are some ideas to draw out in discussion.

- **Built heritage/landscape.** Are there overlaps? Can you consider one without considering the other? Or does a distinction between buildings and spaces work well? Where do issues such as setting fit? For the landscape team – what is the boundary of the site – is it easy to define? Did the team address biodiversity? Or if you are working with natural heritage specialists, did the landscape team address the cultural landscape?

- **Collections.** Again, is there a hard line between collections, buildings and spaces? Are all the collections on site (e.g. archives) and if so are they relevant?

- **Time/historical phase.** Hopefully this team will raise some interesting ideas in relation to significance through time; for example, how important are the most recent changes to the heritage asset? What about the earliest phases of the site/asset – are they important? Often this identifies aspects of the heritage that are overlooked.

- **Stakeholders.** When this team feeds back, compare and contrast the kinds of values and issues that they raise. Are they similar or different?

If the group are familiar with more typical ways of looking at heritage through types of value (e.g. architectural, historical, aesthetic etc.), compare and contrast the different approaches. What are the strengths and weaknesses of each? What might the group take away from this activity in terms of their future heritage practice?

❦ 4.4 UNDERSTANDING A HERITAGE ASSET – PHASING

This is an additional activity that is part of the 'Big Picture Step One' in Section 3 because it adds more detail to the understanding of a specific heritage asset. It is very useful if you are working with people with specialist knowledge of the heritage asset or site as this will call on their expertise. The technique used here is commonly used in archaeological analysis of sites or buildings, but it can work for anything that has changed through time.

⠃⠆ *AIM*

As part of the process of understanding a heritage asset, it is useful to articulate the various changes it has undergone through time.

⠃⠆ *WHAT TO DO*

Start with a new piece of paper. Ask the group to:

Describe the history of the site or heritage from its very earliest times to the present day.

PHASE 0 - underlying geology,
(millions of years) streams, landscape.

PHASE 1 - traditional 'Eora' lands
pre 1780 evidence for early
occupation and trade.

PHASE 2 - first house built by
c. 1813 - John Smith - early contact
1850s with Eora. Farmland.

PHASE 3 - Jones family acquire farm.
late 19th Bill Jones is a politician.
Builds mansion.

PHASE 4 - Family lose money - farm divided -
20th used as convalescent hospital
century after World War One and later
orphanage.

PHASE 5 - House and farm acquired by
1970s - National Parks service because
now of the important biodiversity.
House neglected. Local group
collect stories about place and
want to conserve it.

As they talk, try to organize information about the history of the site into major phases (e.g. construction, or the first period of major alteration).

Give each phase a date range and heading. Ask about the very earliest aspects such as the underlying geology, as well as any evidence of pre-historic occupation that may not be recorded in written evidence. Ensure that the history comes up to the present day; for example, ask about the twentieth-century aspects of the site – events during the first and second world wars, for example. The most recent phase is often the one with the best potential for interpretation and community engagement; it can also be the site's most vulnerable phase – the one that people are least likely to understand.

⁙

VARIATION

As a variation you can also explore the stories of a heritage asset from the perspective of different audiences through time. List each of the different people historically associated with the site or asset – for example a historic house might include servants or slaves, the women of the house, workers in the industries that funded its construction, owners, perhaps soldiers who used it as a hospital in wartime or the campaigners who fought to save it, etc. Working in teams, allocate one group of historic people to each and think about how you would research or find out more about that story. I find that this is a particularly powerful way of discovering the 'untold' stories of a heritage place or collection.

⬡ 4.5 CREATE YOUR OWN DEFINITIONS OF VALUE

Most heritage regimes are based on a specific set of heritage values that are used to justify protecting something. For cultural heritage, these values are variations on a broadly common set of themes that will usually be set out in legislation or policy. For the UK, the list might include the following:

- special architectural or historic interest;
- scientific or technological value;
- social or communal value;
- archaeological or evidential values;
- natural values and
- aesthetic values.

Before introducing formal heritage values, this activity provides a chance to try to define concepts of value.

⦚ AIM

To introduce the most commonly used types of heritage values, and to encourage thinking about how they might be defined.

⦚ WHAT TO DO

Either ask the group to help you make a list of each of the different types of heritage values that are used in their field or provide them with a list on the board (adapt it to your own heritage topic or legislative framework). Have the group work in small teams, and give each team one or more of the values. Ask them to:

Come up with an agreed definition of your value/s. Write the definition on a sheet of paper, but do not identify which type of value it is that you are defining.

When the teams have finished, ask everyone to pass their definitions on to a neighbouring team. Can they identify which value it is? Do they agree with the definition?

⦚ DISCUSSION

Ask whether the different types of value overlap. How easy is it to define each value – particularly aesthetic values? What other issues are raised by trying to define values? Who has the knowledge, power or authority to define that type of value? For example, do you need architectural training to define the aesthetic value of buildings? Do you need to be a historian to define historical value? Can only specialist scientists define the value of natural things?

⚜ 4.6 ASSESSING LEVELS OF SIGNIFICANCE – SCORING, THRESHOLDS AND OTHER MEASURES

There are two dimensions to valuing heritage – one is to articulate the different types of values, and the second is to establish some kind of threshold, degree or level of public interest or significance. The latter is often necessary in order to demonstrate that a heritage asset meets the criteria for formal inclusion in a list or schedule, and thus justifies protection or intervention. The degree of significance informs the 'weight' that is given to a heritage asset in planning or decision-making. For example, more care might be taken of a World Heritage Site than an asset of local importance.

This set of activities introduces people to different ways of thinking about levels of significance.

⠿ *AIM*

To introduce different approaches to setting levels or degrees of significance for heritage, and to explore the issues that arise in doing so.

⠿ *PREPARATION*

This is a set of four activities best done in relation to a case study (a site, asset or collection about which the group have some knowledge). Do them after the activities in Section 3, 'The Big Picture', for a specific site, or if you are teaching heritage in general, use the case study you used for 'Time, Space and Stakeholders' (4.3). You will also need a whiteboard or a wall where you can put up at least four sheets of paper – and coloured stickers or little coloured Post-it notes.

⠿ *WHAT TO DO*

Either do each activity all together as a group or divide the group into four teams and give each an activity to do simultaneously.

Start with a general introduction. Thinking about the case study, ask:

> *How would you rate its importance – high, medium or low? Now, would you say it is of local, regional, national or global importance? And would you say that it is very rare or at risk?*

Did everyone agree or not? The next step is to set the scene for the activities, which explore these issues in more detail, using different heritage values.

⁑ 4.6.1 SCORING SIGNIFICANCE

As a start, make a list of heritage values on the board. I have used the ones that are most commonly used to designate cultural sites and monuments:

- Architectural
- Aesthetic
- Archaeological
- Communal or social
- Historic
- Natural

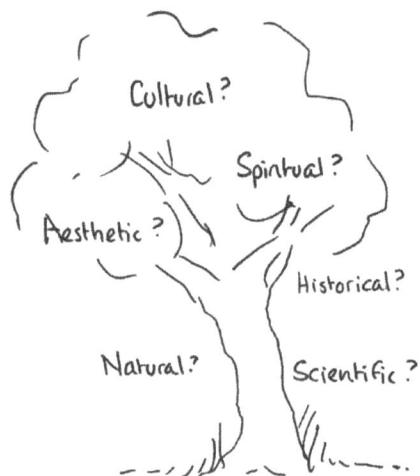

Thinking about the case study, ask everyone in the room to look at the list of values on the board. For each value, they should:

Give the heritage asset a score from 1 to 10 for each value, where 10 is highly significant and 0 is not significant at all.

Ask people to work individually. Keep things moving, and don't let people spend too long on this. Once they have done that, go round the room asking what each score was. Write up each person's score against the type of value.

Type of Heritage Value	Significance Score
Example	*6, 8, 5, 4*
Architectural	
Aesthetic	
Archaeological	
Communal or social	
Historic	
Natural	
Scientific	

How do the scores vary? To what extent did the group agree? Where were the differences? Which values had the biggest range? Think about the issues for each different value – in particular aesthetic value. Can you score it? Open up a discussion on whether you think it is useful to score significance. Maybe take a vote.

Some jurisdictions also include 'Spiritual Value' in the criteria for heritage, so you could also add that into any of these activities.

⠿ 4.6.2 THRESHOLDS OF SIGNIFICANCE

This activity introduces the different thresholds of significance or public interest that are commonly used in heritage designation (you may need to vary this for the type of heritage that you are using, or the country/legislative framework in which you are operating). Those thresholds are usually whether something is of 'local' or 'national' significance or, in the case of World Heritage, 'global' significance (Outstanding Universal Value).

Refer back to the case study and the chart showing heritage values and their scores at beginning of the activity, and ask:

Thinking about the heritage case study, decide the threshold of significance for each heritage value. Is that value of personal, local, regional, national or global significance?

Ask everyone to assign each value with a Post-it note or coloured dot specifying a specific threshold.

Threshold of Significance	Explanation
Outstanding universal value	Is it of global importance for this reason?
National importance	Is it important to the nation as a whole for this reason?
Regional or state importance	Is it important to the region or to the state for this reason?
Local importance	Is it only important to the local parish or area for this reason?
Personal importance	Is it only of importance to a person or family for this reason?

⠿ *DISCUSSION*

Explore how easy it was to define the collective threshold or degree of significance. Think about how easy it is to do for a whole heritage site/landscape/collection as opposed to individual elements. Did they broadly agree or were there big differences? What are some of the factors that people took into account in their decisions? Did things like rarity or accessibility affect their judgement? How else might you capture the collective value or public interest of something?

⁝⁝· 4.6.3 RARITY, INTACTNESS AND OTHER MEASURES OF SIGNIFICANCE

There are a range of other ways to measure degrees or levels of significance that relate mainly to the context or condition of the asset. These are mostly used in biodiversity and natural species conservation but are also used for built and other kinds of heritage.

Once again, ask everyone to see if they can use these as a measure of significance for each of the different heritage values on the board.

Rarity. Is it the only example left?

Intactness. Is the heritage asset in its original condition or relatively unchanged?

Context. Has the context of the asset survived, e.g. setting of a monument, the curtilage of a historic building, the habitat of a species or, for an object, the original packaging?

Threat. To what extent is the heritage at risk or threatened (e.g. priority species, habitats or buildings at risk)?

Age. Is the age of the heritage asset a critical factor for its degree of significance?

⁝⁝· DISCUSSION

Now bring together all four strands into a single table like this, where you use one column for each different way of assessing the degrees of significance.

Heritage Value	Score	Threshold	Measure
Example (architectural)	*6, 8, 5, 4*	*global*	*rarity*
Architectural			
Aesthetic			
Archaeological			
Communal or social			
Historic			
Natural			
Scientific			

Discuss the kinds of issues raised by these different approaches:

- Is there a hard and fast distinction between types of value and degrees of significance?
- How easy is it to set degrees or thresholds?
- What are the problems that arise in doing so?
- Can you define degrees of significance for an asset as a whole or can you only do it for parts of the asset?
- What challenges does defining degrees of significance raise when it comes to managing sites (note that this topic is dealt with in other activities).

❦ 4.7 WHEN EXPERTS COLLIDE 1 – SPECIALIST APPROACHES TO HERITAGE VALUES

Cultural heritage sites and organizations often involve different specialists working together. For example, they might be planners, ecologists, engineers, archaeologists, architects, conservators, museum professionals, or transport heritage experts. As well as different professions, there are different communities of interest. Each of these communities of interest will approach ideas about significance in a different way. Use this activity if you have a mixed group with different backgrounds who all need to work together. It is a version of the 'Professor of Archaeology' activity (2.4).

⠇ *AIM*

To recognize that people with different expertise can see heritage in different ways.

⠇ *PREPARATION*

You will need an object to pass around the room – it could be something simple like a screwdriver.

⠇ *WHAT TO DO*

Pass an object around the room. Ask each person to describe the value of the object from their own expert point of view. For example, if the object is a screwdriver:

- Archaeologist – this can tell me about the history of technology
- Engineer – this is something I can use to fix an engine
- Architect – this is an example of design history
- Curator – this is an artefact that tells us about what people did
- Ecologist – nothing to do with me!
- Academic – all values are relative
- Surveyor – this is not in good condition and needs sharpening
- Anthropologist – this is a symbol of something

If you don't have a wide range of expertise in the room, just ask people to imagine how they think different professional (or indeed community) groups might approach the value of the same object or heritage asset.

⠇ *DISCUSSION*

Draw out the different ways in which people's prior knowledge and expertise impacts on the way they describe the value of a heritage asset. Use that to explore how people from different specialist backgrounds might approach a statement of significance.

❦ 4.8 STATEMENTS OF SIGNIFICANCE
⫶ 4.8.1 STATEMENT OF SIGNIFICANCE – DESIGNATION

This activity explains how to prepare a statement of significance in order to establish whether a heritage asset meets the criteria for inclusion in a formal list (designation).

As 'The "Fried Egg" of Value' (4.2) shows, there is a difference between identifying all the ways in which an asset is valued in order to manage it and assessing whether or not a heritage asset meets the criteria for protection. Protecting or designating a heritage asset involves deciding whether the asset is above or below a particular level or threshold of significance, usually set against formal criteria expressed in legislation policy or guidance. The best known are the criteria for inscription of World Heritage Sites, but most countries or jurisdictions will have their own criteria.

⫶ AIM

To familiarize people with formal significance guidelines, and to apply the lessons learned in earlier exercises to writing a statement of significance.

⫶ PREPARATION

You either need a case study or a site that the group knows something about. You will also need a copy of the relevant criteria for inscription, designation or listing for the jurisdiction in which you work (e.g. the heritage acts or policy documents). For generic teaching purposes, you can also use the World Heritage criteria.

⫶ WHAT TO DO

Provide a copy of the official criteria you are using and an example of something that might be worthy of designation. Either it should be a famous landmark or something well known.

> *Write a statement of significance for the heritage asset using the official criteria. Assess whether it meets the criteria or how it might meet the criteria.*

People will not necessarily have a detailed knowledge of the heritage asset, or of the criteria, so the aim of the exercise is not to get it 'right' but to understand the concept of thresholds and the application of specific criteria.

SORRY – THE BIKE SHED WHERE YOU HAD YOUR FIRST KISS IS JUST NOT NATIONALLY IMPORTANT!

⫶ DISCUSSION

Explore the strengths and weaknesses of the formal criteria for designation. How easy was it to draft a statement of significance using them? Are there values for the heritage that could not be included in the formal designation? If so, what implications might that have in future for how the site is managed?

⁛ 4.8.2 STATEMENT OF SIGNIFICANCE – CONSERVATION MANAGEMENT PLAN

Statements of significance or of heritage values can be written for two different purposes – either to support a case for designation (see above) or to help inform the management of a heritage asset. Heritage sites are usually protected for a fairly narrow range of values, but day-to-day management of places involves recognizing a wider range of values. This was illustrated in 'The "Fried Egg" of Value' (4.2). This activity may be best played after 'Statement of Significance – Designation' (4.8.1) (you may need to adapt it if you use it as a stand-alone activity).

⁛ AIM

To write a statement of significance for management purposes.

⁛ PREPARATION

This requires a case study. Ideally, use the same one that you used to write a statement of significance for designation. If you have done Section 3, refer back to the 'Big Picture Step Four' on management issues.

STRATA FLORIDA ABBEY, RUINED WEST DOOR.

⁛ WHAT TO DO

Ask people to:

> *Think about all of the other ways in which people might value the heritage site over and above those listed in the statement of significance for designation.*

Those values should be in addition to the formal reasons for which the site might be designated. Ask each team to draft some bullet points that might be the basis for a statement of significance that captures those other values.

⁛ DISCUSSION

Ask the teams to compare and contrast the two different statements of significance for designation and management purposes. Do they overlap? Or were they very different. What are the biggest differences? How might those differences affect the way the site is managed?

❦ 4.9 THROUGH THE LENS OF VALUE AND SIGNIFICANCE

As well as being able to articulate heritage values and their significance, anyone who works with natural or cultural heritage needs to understand how assumptions about heritage value and significance inform decision-making and thinking – whether consciously or unconsciously. Here are three activities that demonstrate how our unconscious thinking about value informs what we do. The activities are useful for specialists whose role involves writing or using heritage documents, such as conservators, planners, archaeologists, curators, architectural historians, architects, or people who give out grants, or in environmental assessment. They are also useful for anyone who has to put together a funding application.

⠿ 4.9.1 ANALYSE A CONSERVATION STATEMENT OR MANAGEMENT PLAN

⠿ *AIM*

To show how assumptions about value shape the way we think about heritage.

⠿ *PREPARATION*

You will need a case study and highlighter pens. The case study should be an example of a heritage document, such as a conservation management plan, grant application, development application, strategic plan or project proposal. Remove any pages that are specifically about value or significance, such as a statement of significance, if it exists, and keep them to one side. Then separate the remaining pages, including the cover and list of contents, and give everyone copies along with a highlighter pen. For a long document, you could give each group a few pages.

⠿ *WHAT TO DO*

Ask people to read the documents and with a highlighter pen mark each phrase or sentence that might tell them something about the value or significance of the place. That information might be explicit or implicit. On the basis of the information in the document,

> *Write down three reasons why you think the site might be significant.*

Give people a few minutes to do this and then ask them to compare their statements with other groups. Bring together the best reasons why the site might be important.

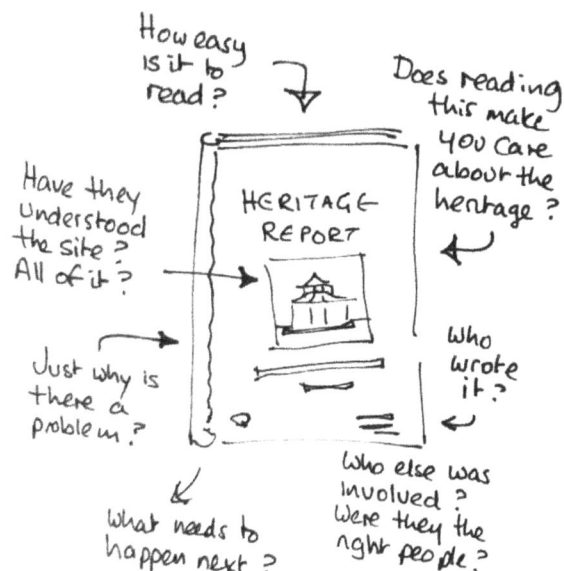

⠿ *DISCUSSION*

Pull out some of the different views on the value or significance of the asset from around the room and discuss the fact that assumptions about significance often underlie the way we write or think. Look at the number of ways in which significance was hinted at or implied within the pages of the document, and how those assumptions have shaped the document and its recommendations. At the end, if there is a formal statement of significance in the original document, share it with the group in hard copy or electronically and ask them to spend a short time reading it.

⠞ 4.9.2 THROUGH THE LENS OF VALUE AND SIGNIFICANCE – MAKE A FUNDING DECISION

This is another activity that helps people to read a heritage document. I use it to teach heritage skills, but it also illustrates how assumptions about significance inform people's actions.

⠞ *AIM*

To teach critical skills to people who read or write planning or conservation documents, or funding applications.

⠞ *PREPARATION*

In advance of the workshop, you will need to prepare a written case study to hand out on the day. It should be a document of about five pages or so, with images. The document could be any planning document – such as a funding application, a conservation statement, a heritage impact assessment, an interpretation plan, a project proposal, a business plan that involves a heritage asset or a corporate plan for a heritage organization. This activity works better if you anonymize a real document rather than create a fake document. I use a short conservation statement submitted with a funding application.

⠞ *WHAT TO DO*

Explain to people that they have been promoted to the role of Grants Officer (or Planning Officer or other relevant decision-maker, depending upon the case study you are using).

Your job will be to decide whether to fund/approve the project or plan, based on a written document.

Explain the context of the document they have been given and its purpose. For example, 'this document has been submitted by an applicant in support of a planning application'. Set a strict time limit (perhaps no more than 10 minutes) to read the document. While they are reading the document, write up a series of questions on the board at the front (I do it while people are reading as it can be daunting to see all the questions written in advance).

Once you have read it, and before you can make a decision, you will need to consider the questions on the board.

These are the questions I use to help the group read a conservation statement:

- Who wrote the document? Why did they write it?
- Is it easy to read?
- Who else was involved – did they consult anyone?
- Have they fully understood the site/collection/heritage as it is now?
- Are there any gaps? Does it include all of the different types of heritage?
- Does the document help you to understand what is important?
- Does it inspire a reader to care about the heritage or understand why it is important?
- What are the issues being faced?
- Is the site/collection/heritage sustainable in the long term? If not, why not?
- What management actions should be taken?

Ask people to discuss the questions briefly with a partner.

⁛ DISCUSSION

Use the list of questions to prompt further questions. On the example I use, there are crucial details missing, so I ask things like 'what is the building made of'. If the group can't answer the question with the information given, I ask whether it matters that they can't.

Prompt the group to think about what might make the document better. What other information would help? A list of contents, bullet points or more illustrations or a summary? After spending some time working through these issues, ask one final question:

> *Would you say yes or no to the applicant?*

If people are not willing to fund the applicant, have a broader discussion about why that is and what might help the applicant to make a better case.

Conclude the exercise by stressing that we all write documents but we don't always think about our readers and that hopefully the exercise has provided some tips. If the group is commissioning a plan, talk to them about what they need in the brief and what they can expect from a consultant.

[Handwritten note: Tip: the key to a successful funding application... is to learn to think like a funder.]

⠿ 4.9.3 REVIEW A HERITAGE REPORT

This exercise is designed for people whose role involves writing or reviewing heritage documents such as

- a business plan for a heritage site
- an options appraisal
- a report in support of a planning application
- a conservation plan
- a disability access statement
- a heritage impact assessment
- an application for a grant or funding
- an application to list or protect something
- a project proposal

The critical questions centre on whether the writer has understood the value of the heritage and how that has informed decisions and recommendations. A 'good' heritage recommendation is one that respects and does not diminish what is important about the site whilst still delivering other outcomes for people.

⠿ AIM

To compare different approaches to a particular heritage issue and also to understand how the way we articulate value and significance informs those approaches.

⠿ PREPARATION

You will need several different examples of heritage reports (e.g. grant applications, or conservation statements or impact assessments). You may need to edit or cut down the reports so they can be used in a teaching session. In advance of the workshop, identify the number of people you will have in the room. Aim to have one different example for each team (say 4–5 people) and enough copies so that everyone can read it.

⠿ WHAT TO DO

Give each team a different report and explain that they are all members of a consultancy firm. The firm that they belong to has prepared this report, but the person who wrote it is on leave, so at the last minute, your team has been asked to present the findings to the client. Ask each team to read the report and appoint a spokesperson:

> *Your spokesperson should make a short presentation to everyone, explaining how you approached the problem, briefly what your recommendations are and why your proposal should be approved.*

Each presentation should be no more than 3 minutes.

⠿⠄ *DISCUSSION*

As facilitator, decide which is the best presentation. You could also vote on or at least debate the merits of each. Compare and contrast the different approaches of each team to the heritage issue. What were the strengths and weaknesses of each? Which were the most convincing? What have they learned from the activity that might enable them to make a stronger application for funding or to write a more convincing application to list or protect something? How did underlying assumptions about heritage value and significance come out in each report?

⚜ 4.10 VALUE AND SIGNIFICANCE – WHO DECIDES?

One of the most common questions that people ask in relation to values-based heritage is 'Who decides?' In other words, who has the final say over what is selected to be collective (rather than personal) heritage and how it is managed? At its most basic, this question is about authority to determine degrees of significance. That determination is what justifies public funding and inclusion in a list or what underpins decision-making. It also forms the basis of the allocation of resources such as funding. So it is in part a question about power and authority, but it is also about how what is collectively important is articulated.

⠿ *PREPARATION*

Whilst this question could arise at any point in almost any of the activities in this book, a group will have a more constructive discussion if they have become familiar with different kinds of value after working through some of the other activities in this section. Use one of the tables you created earlier as a basis for this activity and provide copies for the group.

⠿ *WHAT TO DO*

Ask:

- Who decides on significance?
- How do they decide?
- When do they decide?

If you want to make the discussion more specific, work through each value in the table that you created at the end of activity 4.6.3. Add a final column in for 'who decides'?

Heritage Value	Score	Threshold	Measure	*Who decides?*
Example (architectural)	*6, 8, 5, 4*	*global*	*degree of intactness*	*architectural historian?*
Architectural				
Aesthetic				
Archaeological				
Communal or social				
Historic				
Natural				
Scientific				

⠿ *DISCUSSION*

Open up a wider debate about authority in heritage – and how decisions are made for your area.

5

······
♦

HERITAGE VALUES IN DESIGN, CONSERVATION AND PLANNING DECISIONS

This section contains activities that show how understanding the value of a heritage asset helps inform decisions about new work. Together, the activities illustrate the process of 'heritage impact assessment'. The heritage impact assessment process involves reconciling conflicting values. Somebody wants to do something that will create or deliver one kind of value (such as building a new road) but it will impact on something that has another kind of value (e.g. wildlife).

LOOKING AFTER HERITAGE INVOLVES WEIGHING UP <u>BOTH</u> VALUES + RISKS

Almost all heritage management is about dealing with conflicts of value: development and conservation, profit and amenity, communities and conservators, bats and buildings etc. Those conflicts are not always benign – historic places around the world have sparked riots and even war between different cultural groups. That being said, conflicts can also be good – the genesis of an interesting creative solution may be found in the mayhem of conflicting values.

Rather than avoiding a conflict and hoping it will go away, it is more constructive to wholeheartedly embrace that conflict. Expect it, anticipate it and explore it. And the pathway into those conflicts is through understanding the different values that people hold.

The ability to assess the impact of a proposal on the heritage and to articulate the risks it might involve is vital for planners, architects, archaeologists or engineers, or anyone who is involved in making

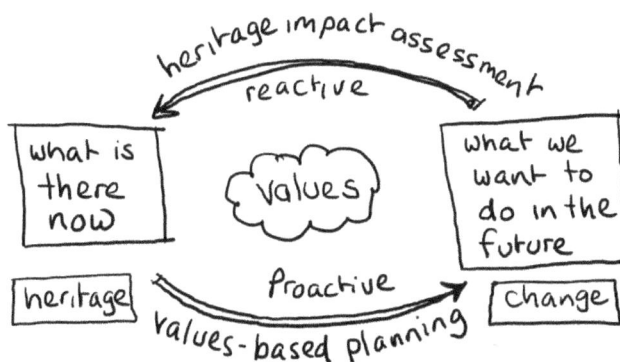

decisions about heritage assets. As with Section 3, 'The Big Picture', these activities can either be used with a case study to engage people in decisions about a particular place or site or they can be used to teach heritage concepts.

The activities in this section focus on risks and benefits to heritage rather than on assessment of the wider economic, social or other benefits of the proposal, which is a separate issue (and requires different skills and knowledge). In the context of decisions about major developments in the planning system, heritage impact is one of many issues that decision-makers need to take into account, but the better the heritage issues are understood at the outset, the less likely they are to create problems or costs later on.

❦ 5.1 DECISION-MAKING STARTER – ARE YOU FOR OR AGAINST?

The best place to start is with the idea that there can be at least two sides to every heritage argument. This is a short introductory activity to use before you then go on to teach or think about impact assessment, risk or mitigation in a more technical and structured way.

AIM

To introduce the idea that heritage decisions very rarely involve a simple yes/no answer.

WHAT TO DO

Ask everyone to:

> *Brainstorm a list of different heritage proposals that might be controversial.*

REINTRODUCING WILD BOAR...
Good idea? Bad idea? or
maybe, depending ....

They should either be real examples or examples of things that might well happen. Try to use real places that people have some knowledge of, such as a local landmark, rather than generic places such as 'an old building'. For example, you might use:

- constructing a tall building next to a major icon such as St Paul's Cathedral in London or the Sydney Opera House
- restoring an original piece of Chippendale furniture
- repainting the cell that Nelson Mandela used at Robben Island
- restoring a church to an earlier phase
- reintroducing a wild species to an area where they are extinct
- getting a vintage car, locomotive or historic ship going again
- cutting down trees in a park
- organizing a major public event at a heritage site

Write the list up on the board. Now run through each item on the list and ask:

> *What do you think of each proposal? Put up your hand if it is*
>
> *1. A good idea*
>
> *2. A bad idea*
>
> *3. Maybe, depending*

Count the scores as you go through the list. How many in each? Were there a lot of 'maybe, dependings?'

⁂ 5.2 HERITAGE IMPACT ASSESSMENT – FIVE QUESTIONS

Like 'The Big Picture', Section 3, this activity involves working through a series of questions that need to be answered in order to make a heritage decision. The process can be used to explore the potential impact of a new proposal on an important heritage asset. Therefore it can be used to consult with a community or with people who want to make their views about a heritage issue known. It can also be used by anyone working in heritage – curators, conservators, land managers – to think about the impact of a new proposal. The questions are:

Question One. What exactly is proposed, and what is the justification for it?

Question Two. What impact will it have on the heritage and its value to people? Is that impact beneficial or harmful?

Question Three. If the project will harm heritage, are there ways of reducing (or mitigating) that harm?

Question Four. For each of the above questions – do you have sufficient information to answer it?

Question Five. If you have sufficient information, are you now able to make a recommendation? And if that recommendation is a qualified 'yes' – are there any conditions required to mitigate harmful impacts?

⁝ *AIM*

To work through a linked set of activities that together illustrate the process of values-based heritage decision-making and introduce ideas such as mitigation.

⁝ *PREPARATION*

These activities work best if based on an actual case study. The case study should be an example of a proposal for a new project or development that might affect a heritage asset. Choose one that is relevant to the people you are working with and that could result in a mixture of benefit and harm to the heritage and its value, whether to the local community or others. You will need some basic information about the proposal, some images and some information about the heritage asset. Present the case study at the beginning of the workshop.

⁞⁝⁞· 5.2.1 WHAT IS THE PROPOSAL AND WHAT IS THE JUSTIFICATION FOR IT?

The first step in the impact assessment process is to understand exactly what is proposed – and the justification for it. The better you understand the proposal, the easier it is to understand its impact.

⁞⁝⁞· *AIM*

To demonstrate the first step in the impact assessment process (which is to be clear about what is proposed).

⁞⁝⁞· *WHAT TO DO*

Work in two teams. One team are the 'Developers' and the other team are the 'Heritage team'. Present the case study, or talk the group through what you know about the proposal.

Tell the 'Developers' to spend a few minutes planning and justifying their project in more detail – what will happen? What will be involved? Why do they need to do it? What are the future economic, social and environmental benefits of the project? The 'Heritage team' should have a few minutes to work out what they need to know about the proposal in order to understand the specific issues relating to heritage. Now give the 'Heritage team' free rein to question the 'Developers' about the project – the aim is to get enough information about what is proposed to begin the heritage impact process. By the end of this step, the 'Heritage team' should have a good understanding of what the project will involve and the justification for it.

⁞⁝⁞ 5.2.2 WHAT WILL BE THE IMPACT ON THE HERITAGE, AND IS THAT BENEFICIAL OR HARMFUL?

This next step explores the concept of 'impact' in more detail and shows that it is not usually a simple black and white problem. Some proposals may be highly beneficial and some totally destructive; but most have a mixture of good and bad impacts, and often the less beneficial aspects of a proposal can be mitigated through careful implementation (or indeed good design). Use the proposal from the exercise above as the starting point for this exercise.

⁞⁝⁞ *AIM*

To explore the ways in which a new proposal might benefit or harm heritage.

⁞⁝⁞ *WHAT TO DO*

For this step, everybody should now join the 'Heritage team' working for the Government, Local Council Planning Department or Funding Body. Their job is to advise the Minister, Mayor or Chief Executive on the merits of the proposal and whether or not it should be supported/funded/given consent. But before they can give that advice, they need more information.

Ask each team to set out three columns on a large piece of paper – 'good', 'bad' and 'maybe'.

Thinking about the proposal you have in front of you, identify

1. *Which aspects of it might be beneficial?*
2. *Which might be harmful?*
3. *Which aspects might be neutral?*

Look at both the community, and the heritage.

⁞⁝⁞ *DISCUSSION*

Ask each team to pass their sheets on to the next table or neighbouring team. Ask each team to review the new sheet – do they agree or disagree with the previous team's assessment? What is the balance between good, bad and maybe?

⠿ 5.2.3 DO YOU HAVE SUFFICIENT INFORMATION TO MAKE A HERITAGE DECISION?

Having established that impact is not straightforwardly good or bad, the next step is to ensure that there is sufficient information to better understand that impact. One of the biggest issues in decision-making is the quality of the information on which to base it.

⠿ *AIM*

To understand the different kinds of information that might contribute to making good decisions about cultural heritage.

⠿ *WHAT TO DO*

Continuing to work through the case study or the specific proposal ask:

> *Consider the information that will enable you to properly assess the impact of the proposal on the heritage. Identify five pieces of information that you will need.*

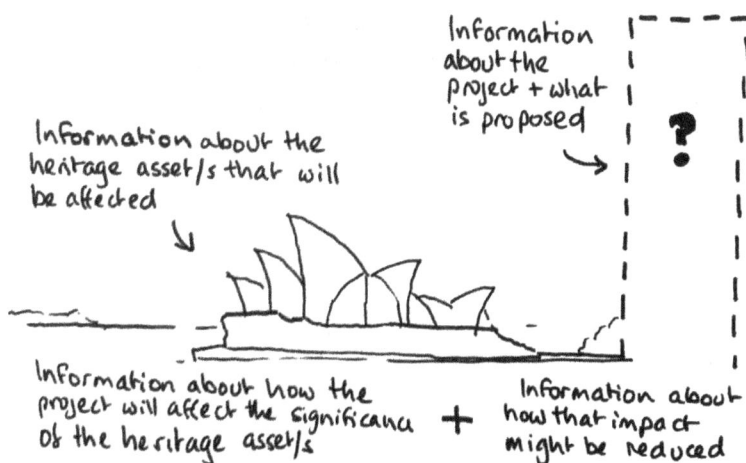

Information about the heritage asset/s that will be affected

Information about the project + what is proposed

Information about how the project will affect the significance of the heritage asset/s

+ Information about how that impact might be reduced

?

Remind them to focus on the *information* you would need and NOT the decision.

⠿ *DISCUSSION*

Discuss the information that might be needed in order to make a decision. On the board, organize the feedback into different kinds of information; there will probably be four kinds that people mention:

- information about the project and what is proposed (e.g. the new scheme or the new building or the restoration proposal)
- information about the heritage item that is affected
- information about what the impact will be or how the new proposal might affect the item and the community – and whether that is beneficial or harmful
- information about ways in which any harmful aspects of that impact on the heritage or the community might be reduced – such as whether there are options to change the design

Ask the group to think about where, how and from whom such information might be sourced – for example, through documentary research, scientific investigation, field survey or archaeology, oral history, engagement with key groups, or technical or design advice.

⠿ 5.2.4 CAN YOU AVOID, MITIGATE OR OFFSET ANY HARMFUL IMPACTS?

I am never
Flying again...

AVOID

Oh ok,
maybe I'll
only fly
occasionally...

MITIGATE

I give up!
I'll fly, but
plant a tree
as well

OFFSET

The next concept is the idea of 'mitigation' – how the potential harm to cultural heritage values that might arise in any new project or proposal can be reduced in order to deliver wider community benefits. If you have been working through these steps in order, by now the group should be aware that the majority of issues affecting a significant thing or place are not either beneficial or harmful but a mixture of both.

As colleagues in natural heritage management are well aware, the way to minimize harm is through some form of mitigation strategy. Whilst this language is less often used for cultural heritage assets – let alone intangible ones – the process is similar. The process of reducing harm to heritage whilst also delivering other benefits is also a core part of the process of designing in a historic context.

⠿ *AIM*

To explain the concept of mitigation and some of the key ways in which potential harm to heritage places can be reduced.

⠿ *PREPARATION*

You will need the list of potential ways in which the new proposal might harm the heritage asset that the group developed in activity 5.2.2 (above). For example, there might be harm to the surrounding area, to buried archaeology or to the heritage asset itself. You will also need to prepare a series of cards, each which a different mitigation strategy written on it. You will need a set of cards for each team. For example, the cards might say:

Avoid	Mitigate	Offset
don't do it at all	choose different materials	make a record of what was there
do it another way	redesign the new work to lessen impact	create an equivalent benefit somewhere else
just let it fall down	make the new work very different to the old work	use some of the profits to achieve a different heritage benefit
repair the heritage building and reuse it	restore it	create public access
put in place a maintenance regime	provide public interpretation	repair a different heritage asset using the profits
manage the site in a particular way	put conditions on the new work	
do the same thing somewhere else	use a different technique	
	the new work is reversible	

⠿· *WHAT TO DO*

Ask the teams to work through the list of different ways in which the new proposal might harm the heritage. Get them to use the cards to see if they can identify some way of reducing the damaging impact of the new proposal through avoiding, mitigating or offsetting any harm. Teams can set it out as a table like this:

Potential Harm	Card	Possible Ways to Avoid/Mitigate/Offset Harm
Example: The new tall building will have a negative effect on views of the city from the Opera House	*Mitigate – redesign the new work to lessen impact* *Avoid – do the same thing somewhere else* *Offset – use the profits to achieve a different heritage benefit*	*– Reduce the height of the new building or look at design changes* *– Create new apartments somewhere else in the city* *– Use profit from the new building to better maintain the Opera House*

⠇⠇ *DISCUSSION*

Ask each team to present their mitigation strategies. How do they compare in their approach? Which mitigation strategies were the most useful? Which are ok but would not reasonably mitigate a harm? Ask the group as a whole:

> *Do you think it is possible to mitigate the harm done by the new proposal? Overall, do the benefits outweigh the harm, given any mitigation strategies?*

VARIATION

The extent to which a developer may or may not feel able to incorporate the mitigation strategy into the design of the proposal will in part depend upon their assessment of the costs and feasibility of those strategies. The teams could now switch hats to become the 'Developers' again. What do you think of the suggestions that the 'Heritage team' have made? Are they feasible or affordable? Are there any benefits to you in addressing these issues?

⣿ 5.2.5 MAKE THE DECISION AND SET CONDITIONS

But there is one critical thing missing – after all of this analysis, should we say 'yes' or 'no' to the proposal? Are there any conditions that might ensure that it is a good decision?

⣿ AIM

To use the information in the exercises above to make a decision and identify any conditions.

⣿ WHAT TO DO

Start by writing the following on the board:

> Yes – the project should go ahead because any harm to the value of cultural heritage is outweighed by the wider benefits that it will deliver.

> No – the project should not go ahead, because any good is outweighed by the harm to the value of the cultural heritage.

> Maybe – the project should probably go ahead if it can meet certain conditions that will reduce any harm to the wider value of the heritage.

Ask the group:

> *In view of the potential benefit and harm to the heritage and to the community, would you advise that the project go ahead?*

If the decision is 'Yes, go ahead with the project, but . . .' ask:

> *What conditions or requirements might be placed on the developer in order to ensure that the development can go ahead in a way that is least damaging to the heritage?*

Ask each team to review the various mitigation strategies that they think might reduce the harm of the proposal. Is it possible to boil those down into a few 'conditions'? Note that drafting conditions is a specialist skill. Most planning jurisdictions have clear requirements on what conditions can be imposed on a development and how they should be worded. In UK Planning Policy, the six tests for planning conditions are that they should be:

1. necessary,
2. relevant to planning and,
3. to the development to be permitted,
4. enforceable,
5. precise and,
6. reasonable in all other respects.

The policy notes that conditions should not be used, for example, to unreasonably impact on the delivery of a development, or to require payment of money (although it is possible to require a development to not go ahead until something is done).

⬤ 5.3 PUT IT ALL TOGETHER – MAP YOUR OWN HERITAGE DECISION-MAKING PROCESS

This activity is another technique for teaching the idea of a 'heritage impact assessment'. You can use it on its own, or you can use it after you have worked through the steps above. In this activity, you are asking people to come up with their own map of how to make a heritage decision.

⠿ *AIM*

To teach people about the principles of heritage decision-making by asking them to map the process in their own way.

⠿ *PREPARATION*

You will need a large sheet of paper and some Post-it notes.

⠿ *WHAT TO DO*

Ask the group to think about how heritage decisions are made. Ask them to:

> *Write a list of questions that you would need to answer in order to make a heritage decision.*

If you have done the steps above, use that exercise as a starting point. Otherwise, think about a particular heritage decision that they might need to make. Ask each team to write each question on a Post-it note and arrange them into a logical order on the big sheet of paper.

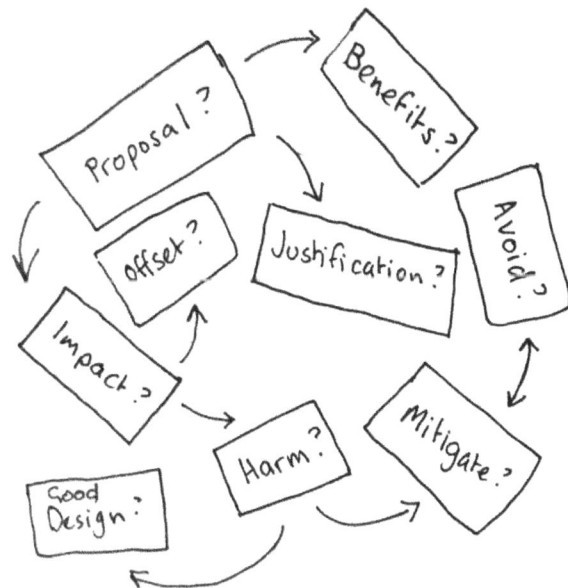

⠿ *DISCUSSION*

Ask each team to present their process. Compare the different processes. What are the similarities? What are the differences? Can you come up with a single process?

✾ 5.4 EXPLORE IMPACT IN MORE DETAIL – USE A HERITAGE IMPACT TABLE

This is another approach to thinking about heritage impact. It puts some of the information above into a table format. It can be useful if you have a complex project with many different elements. If you have done some of the previous activities indoors, do this one on site.

AIM

To develop a structured approach to assessing the impact of a project or proposal on a heritage site.

PREPARATION

Before the group go on site, present a specific proposal for consideration. For example, if you are at a museum, the proposal might be for a new extension; if it is a locomotive, the proposal might be to restore it to full working order; if it is a country park or wildlife site, the proposal might be to build a new visitor centre. Prepare copies of the table below, to be filled in after the site visit.

Proposal Set out all the work that the new proposal will involve	Values or Significance For each element of the project, identify what might be affected and why it is important	Impact on Significance or Value What will be the impact of each aspect of the project and is it beneficial or harmful?	Mitigation For each aspect of the project that might have a harmful effect on significance, is there a practical mitigation strategy?

░· WHAT TO DO

Send people out to the site to examine the new proposal. Ask them to:

> *Look at the heritage now and think about all the different things that might be affected by the new proposal. What are the benefits of the new proposal? What are the drawbacks? How can any negative impacts or risks be reduced or avoided?*

Back in the workshop, draw a version of the table on the whiteboard at the front. Using your case study, fill in a couple of rows yourself, talking through each heading in turn. Put people into teams and ask them to fill in their copy of the table.

░· DISCUSSION

If you have done the earlier activities in this section, the group should be able to fill in the table relatively easily. They should have the confidence to think about impact and identify potential mitigation strategies.

5.5 CLOSER – WHAT MAKES A GOOD HERITAGE DECISION?

Having worked through some of the activities in this section, it may be useful to have a general discussion about what makes a good heritage decision.

WHAT TO DO

Divide into two teams again. Once again, one team should be the 'Developers' and the others should be the 'Heritage' team. Ask each team:

What are your top five criteria for a good heritage decision?

Those criteria might be to do with the outcome, the process, the quality of information or the way the decision is made.

DISCUSSION

Compare and contrast the different approaches. Do the Developers have a different set of criteria to the Heritage team?

6

VALUES IN VISITOR MANAGEMENT – ENGAGING WITH AUDIENCES

The activities in this section are designed for museums, parks and other organizations (or owners) who want to interpret heritage places that are open to the public. They are all about how people engage with heritage sites or collections and are designed to help develop new public programmes or interpretation services, or improve access.

Don't forget that interpretation is not just about signs or panels – it is all of the different ways in which people connect with heritage. 'Hard' interpretation includes physical things such as guidebooks, leaflets, signage and screens. 'Soft' interpretation is all of the other ways that people connect with heritage sites and museums, such as events and public programmes, storytelling, activities for people of all ages, talks and presentations, and opportunities to get involved.

Heritage values are as critical to interpretation as they are to cultural heritage protection and management. The National Lottery Heritage Fund in the UK says of interpretation:

> It is not just about facts and figures. It is the way in which the interest, value, significance and meaning is communicated to people. It is a learning activity which communicates the stories and ideas behind the heritage and provokes the audience to think for themselves, coming to their own understanding about what the subject means to them.[1]

Interpretation is as much about sharing stories and making those personal and emotional connections as it is about sharing facts and information.

---

1. Heritage Lottery Fund, 'Interpretation – Good-Practice Guidance', April 2013, p. 3, https://www.heritagefund.org.uk.

⚜ 6.1 STARTER – ACCESS OR PARTICIPATION?

One of the tricky debates I have often had is around the difference between access and involvement (or participation). The first is where you visit a site or museum (or website) and the second is where you play an active role in doing something – it is the difference between passive and active engagement.

AIM

To flag the difference between 'access' and 'participation' or involvement.

PREPARATION

Have a supply of small blank cards. Ideally, they should be roughly the same size as a playing card. You need around 20 or 30 for each team.

WHAT TO DO

Give each team a pile of cards. Ask them to brainstorm different things that people might do in relation to a heritage site and write one on each card, for example, see an exhibition; climb a tower; volunteer; drive a steam engine; go on a guided walk.

Ask them to try to sort the cards into two groups – one marked 'access' and one marked 'participation'? Do cards fit easily into one or the other? Are there lots in the middle? Alternatively, the cards can be lined up as a sequence, with 'passive' at one end and 'active' at the other.

DISCUSSION

Have a brief discussion about the difference between heritage activities that are all about access and activities that involve people. Are they very different or is there a spectrum? What does this mean if you are planning activities on a site?

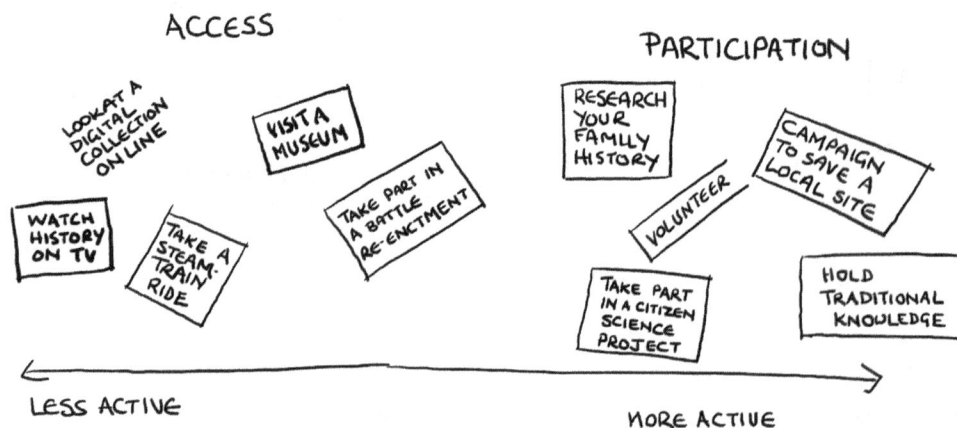

6.2 ACCESS TO HERITAGE – WE ALL EXPERIENCE BARRIERS

This activity underlines the point that access is not just an issue for people who happen to use wheel-chairs – anyone can face access barriers. It also shows that experiencing access problems is not just irritating but often humiliating and frustrating and can affect the whole experience so you don't want to return and certainly would not recommend the site to friends.

AIM

To demonstrate that everyone can experience barriers to accessing heritage, regardless of ability or circumstances.

WHAT TO DO

Ask everyone in the room to:

> *Think of a recent example of where you visited (or wanted to visit) a heritage site or place and had a problem with access.*

Explain that they don't have to be a wheelchair user to have encountered problems with access. It could have been a matter of getting a stroller bogged down in a sandy path or not being able to work out the opening times from a website.

> *Think about three things:*

- *What was the problem?*
- *How did it make you feel?*
- *What would you have liked the organization to have done?*

Quickly go around the room asking for everyone's stories.

DISCUSSION

Ask people:

> *Do you have to be disabled to experience barriers? What are the different kinds of barriers that we heard about during the feedback?*

You might prompt people to think about the following barriers:

Intellectual	Sensory	Physical
Cultural	Financial	Organizational

Highlight any types of access that have not already been identified, and ask people to think of examples.

⬚ 6.3 TRY IT FOR YOURSELF – EXPERIENCING BARRIERS

How people experience a heritage site is a key part of its value for them, but such 'experiential' values are often overlooked in discussions about significance.

⠿ *AIM*

To give people a physical experience of barriers, and thus some insight into challenges and possible remedies.

⠿ *PREPARATION*

This exercise should be done at a heritage site with access to a classroom or quiet space for pre- and post-activity briefing. Check in advance with the staff that they are comfortable for participants to be on site, especially if it is open to the public. You may need a risk assessment.

In advance, gather together whatever equipment you can find that may result in access issues – a stroller, a blindfold or simply a pair of headphones that cut out most sound, a pair of crutches, a walking stick. Perhaps ask whether anyone is prepared to bring a toddler along for the day!

If you agree it in advance, you could also ask the museum/site staff or volunteers if they would like to come into the classroom for the feedback (or even participate in the workshop). Ask them to talk about how they manage access issues.

⠿ *WHAT TO DO*

Start in the classroom. Working in pairs, one person should be designated 'able' and the other 'disabled' (or 'differently abled'). Hand out the equipment listed above (or allocate responsibility for the toddler!)

> *You have a disability for a day. You also may have a more able helper. Please make a quick visit to the site/museum and capture your impressions of the experience. Make sure you check out the toilet/cafe/interpretation. You must be back in [half an hour].*

⠿ *DISCUSSION*

Back in the workshop, ask each pair to spend a short time preparing their feedback. What barriers did they face? And what would have made things easier? Capture the key points on the board and discuss not just the barriers that people faced but the way people felt about them, and therefore the impact that had on their overall experience. If anyone has day-to-day personal experience dealing with significant access challenges, ask them to lead the discussion or provide feedback on the issues identified by the group.

6.4 KIDS TAKEOVER DAY

Why not stage a day for children (or indeed anyone else) to take over a heritage site or museum? Kids in Museums is a UK organization that encourages children to take over sites. It has a website and resources to help plan a day. This section is not strictly an activity but instead provides some suggestions about what such a day might include. Adapt it to deliver different activities for different audiences.

AIM

To enable people to plan a 'Kids Takeover Day'.

PREPARATION

Step One – Connect

Start by connecting with some young people (or your target audience) – they could be visitors, a local school or a youth group or organization, or simply put up a poster to recruit people. Talk to them about how best to make arrangements to visit your site – establish what lead up time they need, who needs to accompany them, how many can come and the rough age of the children.

Step Two – Plan Logistics

Decide whether to do the day when the site is open or closed – either can work. Double check that the day does not coincide with maintenance or other events. Review safety and security, including first aid and evacuation procedures. Plan for supervision on the day. Ensure that you have access to toilets, lunch arrangements and, if needed, bag storage.

Step Three – Choose the Activities

The next step is to plan activities, ideally in consultation with the young people. Examples of the kinds of things that they could do are:

- be a director for a day – appoint young people to key roles in the shop, on site
- design a new activity such as a family trail or quiz
- deliver an activity, such as a tour
- give feedback on the site's website
- help with basic maintenance or inspecting the site
- design a new play area
- put on a short play or storytelling event for their parents or other visitors

Step Four – Finalize the Plan

Put it all together into a plan for the day – timings, activities, health and safety, materials and arrangements. Share the plan with the young people in advance.

WHAT TO DO

Deliver the day!

DISCUSSION

After the day, talk to the children and staff/supervisors about how it went. What lessons can you learn for next time?

⚏ 6.5 LOOKING FOR MYSELF – FIND YOUR OWN STORY

One of the most powerful factors in interpreting a heritage site is the ability for audiences to connect to its places or stories. People don't always want a lecture about history – or if they do, it is often so they can make a connection to some area of history that they know about. More often, visitors connect with their own personal stories. The exercises in Section 1 such as 'My Heritage, Your Heritage' and 'Who Am I?' are also relevant to this.

⚏ *AIM*

This exercise is designed for participants who may be developing interpretation strategies. It emphasizes the role of personal connections to heritage places.

⚏ *PREPARATION*

If possible, do this activity on site or at a museum. Failing that, use a website, leaflet or other piece of interpretation as a case study. Everyone should use the same thing.

⚏ *WHAT TO DO*

Ask everyone to work individually.

> *On your own, explore the site (or review the website or interpretation material). Look for connections between yourself and the heritage interpretation.*

Give people a strict time limit, and ask them to note down up to five connections.

THOSE ROSES REMIND ME OF MY GRANDMOTHER

⚏ *DISCUSSION*

Back in the classroom, ask:

- How easy was it to make connections?
- Could everyone find five connections?
- What types of things were you able to connect to – family? Experiences? Knowledge? Possessions? Stories?
- What was your personal response?
- How did the museum's approach to interpretation compare with your own personal connections – were they the same or different?
- Do you feel differently about the site or museum having made a personal connection?

VARIATION

If you are developing an interpretation strategy for a particular site or museum, use types of connection to map out some of the stories with which people will connect.

⚛ 6.6 THE 100-WORD STORY

Storytelling is the key to good interpretation, but it can be quite challenging to tell a story well and concisely. This exercise helps people develop written or verbal storytelling skills, whilst the variation below helps them to connect with audiences.

⠿· *AIM*

To help participants develop storytelling skills.

⠿· *WHAT TO DO*

Ask everyone in the room to think of one topic that they know a lot about – it could be anything: their family, the place they grew up, a subject they have studied or a team that they follow.

> *Write a short story about it in no more than 100 words.*

This is about ten lines of text. People don't need to be too fussy about counting words – just keep it short! Give people no more than 10 minutes.

⠿· *DISCUSSION*

Decide how you want to play the feedback. Not everyone will be comfortable about reading out their story, so either ask people to read to their neighbour or ask a couple of volunteers to read theirs out to everyone. Ask listeners for feedback on the story. Does it make sense? Did the listeners get a good sense of the topic in a short time? Did they want to know more? Talk about the challenges of constructing a short story. What makes a story? What are the challenges of writing it in 100 words? Relate the exercise back to the challenges of on-site interpretation. If available, hand out an interpretation leaflet (or refer to a website) and evaluate it in terms of the exercise.

⚛

VARIATION

⠿· *Aim*

To show how you can extract different stories from one place or for one object for different audiences.

⠿· *Preparation*

Start in a classroom or quiet space, then go out to a museum or onto a heritage site or give everyone the webpage for a museum or heritage site.

⁝⁘ *What to Do*

Ask them to start by nominating different audiences – e.g. primary school children, a bowling club, a family or a visitor from another country. Write the name of each audience type on a piece of paper and put it in a hat. Divide the room into teams and ask each to pick an audience out of the hat. Ask each team to go to the museum or onto their website and:

> *Research a story that will interest that audience. Then come back to the classroom and write it up in no more than 100 words.*

⁝⁘ *Discussion*

Come together to share the stories. Focus on the audiences they aimed at rather than the challenge of writing a 100-word story. How different is each audience? Is there an overlap? Which audiences were easiest? Which were hardest?

⚬ 6.7 VOTE FOR MY INTERPRETATION PROJECT!

This exercise is designed to help people think about heritage interpretation – such as public programmes and other activities. Teams develop a site-based heritage activity and present it back. Everyone votes on which activity interprets the site most effectively and sounds the most fun. A heritage activity might be anything that helps people to connect with the site, such as an event, a game, a workshop, a performance, an exhibition or a signboard.

⁞ *AIM*

To enable participants to devise heritage activities that interpret a heritage site effectively.

⁞ *PREPARATION*

If you are in a classroom and not on site, you will need to prepare case studies in advance of the exercise. They should consist of about two sides of paper describing a heritage site or museum, with a picture and a brief account of what it is and what is on offer. Put each into an envelope. There should be one case study for each team of four to five people.

If you are working at a single site or museum, everyone can develop a different activity for the same situation and there is no need for a case study. You will need stickers for voting, as well as a small prize for the winning team (such as sweets). I also use a novelty egg timer.

⁞ *WHAT TO DO*

Explain that:

> *You work for a company that specializes in heritage activities and interpretation. The client has asked you to develop interpretation for their site and enter it into a competition. Only one project in the competition will be funded. The competition will be judged by everyone in the room.*

Ask one representative of each team to pick an envelope (omit this step if you are working on one site). Explain that teams have 25 minutes to develop their project and will be given no more than 3 minutes to present it back. Teams should present their project in any way they like including through drawings or on the flip chart. Keep the pressure up a little by keeping them to time and ringing a bell when time is up. As each team presents, number their project and write down its title on the board.

⁞ *DISCUSSION*

Vote on which project best interpreted the site. You can do this by asking everyone to stick a dot by the one they thought most effective, but this is not very anonymous! Otherwise ask everyone to write down the number of the project they prefer on a slip of paper and put it in a box at the front then count up the votes.

Discuss the factors that make a project successful. Capture these on the board at the front. Give sweets or a small prize to the winning team.

☙ 6.8 MY BEST DAY OUT – CAPTURE YOUR VISITOR EXPERIENCES

This activity involves everyone thinking about the best day that they could have at a specific museum or heritage site and capturing that in words. We used it as part of a museum branding project in order to help us to think more like visitors and less like a curators.

⦂⦂ *AIM*

The aim is to ask people to capture the best words to express the experience of the heritage site or museum in question.

⦂⦂ *PREPARATION*

This is played in a classroom and requires large pieces of paper and felt-tip pens.

⦂⦂ *WHAT TO DO*

Think about a recent visit to the museum or heritage site.

> *In your own words – or thinking about someone you know well, such as a child, parent or friend – describe your/their ideal day out at the museum/heritage site.*

Try to keep to around fifty words or so.

⦂⦂ *DISCUSSION*

Get each person to stand up and read out their statement. Pull out the different viewpoints and experiences. Ask what each participant will take away from the activity.

❦ 6.9 WHAT IS GOOD INTERPRETATION?

What is good interpretation? Whilst this can seem very subjective, the National Heritage Lottery Fund in the UK provides a useful scorecard that can help you explore that issue. This exercise uses that scorecard to review a project.

⠿ *AIM*

To think about what makes good interpretation.

⠿ *PREPARATION*

Ideally, do this activity on site. If that option is not open to you, you could use a website for a museum or even a copy of a leaflet or guidebook.

In advance of the day, type up and print out this checklist. Provide enough copies of it so that each person can have one. Ideally, provide clipboards if you are on site.

	Does it do this? If so, how?	What else could you do?
Catch the attention		
Provide a connection between heritage and people's own experience		
Be pleasurable, interesting, meaningful		
Be well organized and easy to use and understand		
Meet the needs of a variety of audiences		
Have a clear theme or idea to communicate		

⫶· *WHAT TO DO*

Get people to work in pairs. Ask them to go onto the site (or use the website, guidebook or leaflet).

> *On the scorecard, record your impressions of one aspect of the interpretation; for example, a gallery, interpretation board or introductory film.*

As with all exercises on site, set a very tight time limit and enforce it.

⫶· *DISCUSSION*

Have an open discussion of the results of the survey. Ask people to talk about their impressions, and pull out general points about interpretation. If you want to take it a step further, review the scorecard. Does it work? Could you create a better one?

6.10 BE CREATIVE – DEVISE A MUSEUM GAME!

I watched a museum audience play this at the Museums Association conference in Cardiff. It was led by Danny Birchall and Katy Beale, two museum games experts.

AIM

To devise a game based on a heritage asset or museum object, and in doing so make friends.

PREPARATION

You will need to prepare three sets of cards. One set of cards should name a museum object or heritage asset, another should name an activity, and the third set should name a behaviour. You will need enough cards so that each team in the room can pick one card from each set. For example:

> **Museum or heritage object cards** – a medieval sword, The Mona Lisa, Stonehenge
>
> **Activity cards** – hopping, singing, dancing, staying still, shutting your eyes
>
> **Behaviour cards** – getting someone to laugh, win, make friends, finish first, build something

WHAT TO DO

Put the three sets of cards into three different boxes. Ask someone from each team to pick one card from each box. Each team should now devise a game using the three cards they have chosen (an Object card, an Activity card and a Behaviour card). The game that they devise should include a scenario and a set of rules. For example, if a team draws the following three cards: 'The Mona Lisa', 'staying still' and 'making someone laugh', they might devise a game where one person has to be the Mona Lisa and sit very still while everyone else tries to make them laugh. Once each team has devised a game, halt the exercise. Ask each team to explain their game to the next team, who should then play it.

DISCUSSION

Ask people to rate the games that they played. If you have time, get the whole group to play the most highly rated game.

7

VALUES IN DAY-TO-DAY SITE MANAGEMENT

This section contains activities based on the real issues faced by people who look after heritage assets or places that are open to the public as visitor attractions. There are two core aspects to public heritage site management – managing visitors and managing physical things – although inevitably the two overlap.

Managing visitors means providing things like interpretation, activities and public programmes but also providing visitor services such as welcoming people, ticketing, retail and keeping people safe on site.

Managing things involves caring for and conserving collections or the site itself, managing facilities such as toilets, shops, galleries or visitor centres, and keeping the site safe. There are also a wide range of other activities including managing staff, marketing and complying with regulations (such as environmental and health regulations) and overseeing weddings or filming or evening events etc.

As ever, it is a question of reconciling heritage values with other values and benefits. The activities in Section 3, 'The Big Picture', showed how understanding heritage values can help to inform management planning in the broadest sense. The activities in this section are designed to help people apply some of these broad principles to day-to-day practical site management.

⁙ 7.1 THE FIRST FIFTY YARDS (OR METRES)

This activity was inspired by Simon Jenkins, former Chair of the National Trust in the UK, who used to say that if people could not get a sense of the story of a place in the first fifty metres, you had lost them.

⁙ AIM

To think about what people see and experience as they approach a museum or heritage site and how best to enhance their experience (or at least capture their attention).

⁙ PREPARATION

Do this exercise on site at a heritage site or museum, returning to a classroom or workspace afterwards. Don't forget to check in advance with the site managers whether they are happy to do this, especially if it is open to the public. Equip participants with clipboards and paper.

⁙ WHAT TO DO

In the classroom, start by explaining that the purpose of the exercise is to capture first impressions of a heritage site or museum and explore how that influences people's decision to visit. Suggest that people work in teams, and instruct the following:

> *Start at the car park or in the street just near the entrance to the site. Record your first impressions in words or pictures. On the basis of those first impressions, are you going to stop and visit or keep going?*

People can use an annotated sketch, photographs or video, or simply words, to record their impressions. To keep the exercise moving and ensure people are working on first impressions, give people a very short time limit (10–15 minutes).

Back in the classroom, review the pictures and notes. Ask people to feedback five things that they experienced as first impressions.

⠿ *DISCUSSION*

Discuss what people learned or experienced as they came into the site. Does the entrance make you want to come in off the street? Is it welcoming? Were people confident that the site would be of interest and good fun? Finally, ask teams to suggest ways in which (if needed) the site entrance might be improved.

VARIATION

Each team could choose to play a different character or type of visitor e.g.:

- non-English speaking tourists
- a family on holiday in the area
- someone who is taking their elderly father on a day outing
- a local person planning a day out for relatives visiting from overseas
- someone who is looking for something to do with their friends

What might your chosen visitors think about the site? Would they choose to stop and visit? If not – what could be done to make the site more welcoming to them?

⸭ 7.2 IT COULDN'T HAPPEN HERE – DEALING WITH A CRITICAL INCIDENT ON SITE

Anyone who opens a site to the public needs to deal with and be aware of health and safety. Here is a heritage variation of a common health and safety exercise. It involves everyone playing the role of a character and acting out some of the risky issues that could happen at a heritage site as a fun way to approach a risk assessment.

⠇ *AIM*

To help people to identify health and safety issues at a heritage site.

⠇ *PREPARATION*

This exercise takes at least two hours or longer and requires some preparation. It is best played on site such as at a museum or in an outdoor space, although you need to check first whether or not this will interfere with visitor events. If that is not possible, play it in a large room. You will need a whistle or something to make a loud noise and a set of cards.

Most importantly, you will need to spend some time in advance of the exercise creating a scenario, characters and actions (although if you have more time, the group could do that with you). Here is one that you can use as a starting point or adapt for your own ideas:

> **Scenario** – A leader has brought a tour group to the museum or heritage site. They are mainly older people and not all speak English. One person has a visual impairment, and one is a bit confused.

> **Action** – The aim of the leader is to get the tour group from one side of the site to the other (or from one museum gallery to another). En route an incident will occur – in this case a visitor will trip and fall. Things will escalate, and the facilitator (you) will need to stop the exercise. A debrief should follow.

> **Characters** – Each person should be a character and will have a role to play in the incident. On each card, write the name of the character and what they are to do during the incident (or how they are to behave).

The cards/characters could include:

> *The tour leader* – you are in charge of the whole tour group and are responsible for health and safety. If anything happens during the tour, you may call the paramedic.

> *The tour leader's assistant* – you assist the leader but are only allowed to do what they tell you.

> *Museum staff member or site docent/custodian* – you are at the site – you are responsible for the site and ensuring that visitors are safe during their visit.

The assistant docent/custodian – you are at the site, but you must stay at the front desk.

Mrs Smith – you are on the tour. You are in your seventies and quite fit. At a signal from the facilitator a few minutes into the exercise (two blasts of the whistle), you must trip and fall. In the fall you badly injure your foot.

Mr Smith – you are accompanying your wife on the tour. Lately, you have begun to get a bit confused.

Prof. Jones – you are on the tour. You used to work as a historian so you know this site well, but your visual impairment is getting worse.

Mrs Sanchez – you are on the tour. Part way through the scenario at the signal from the facilitator, you develop heart palpitations.

M. Girolle – you are on the tour but do not speak English.

One of the site volunteers – you live locally and are rostered on. You are at the site.

A paramedic – you only appear when called.

Two observers – (optional) you do not take part in the scenario, but you observe what happens from the sidelines.

You may appoint further roles, such as more tour members, depending on the number of people in the group.

WHAT TO DO

Explain what will happen. Each person will draw a card that will tell them their character and what their character will do. They should not share that with others. You the facilitator will direct events. Everyone who is on the tour should begin at one side of the space. People whose characters are on site – the custodian or docent, assistant and the volunteer – should take up their positions. Explain that at:

- **One blast of the whistle** – the tour leader and assistant tour leader should lead the tour group around the site – stopping to see important things. Note that when you blow the whistle three times, the incident should stop.
- **Two blasts of the whistle** – the 'incident' should occur. Allow the incident to progress.
- **Three blasts of the whistle** – the activity should cease.

When everybody is clear about their role, get them into their starting positions. Blow the whistle to begin. Watch the event as it progresses. You may wish to give some additional instructions as it goes along. If (and when!) chaos ensues, blow the whistle to end the scenario.

DISCUSSION

Back in the classroom, discuss the issues that arose. Ask the observers to talk about what they saw. Then ask different tour members for their observations. In small teams, ask people to identify three things that they learned from the event. List these issues and discuss their implications for managing visitors.

7.3 PEOPLE DO THE DARNEDEST THINGS! IDENTIFY RISKS AT A HERITAGE SITE

Anybody who looks after a heritage asset or organizes events at a heritage site will need to be familiar with risk assessment processes. This activity looks at risks to visitors at heritage sites. Whilst a heritage site may be fundamentally dangerous – steep stairs, long drops, slippery surfaces – managing risks is as much about understanding how people behave at a site as about the site itself.

AIM

To develop skills in understanding behavioural aspects of risk assessment as well as identifying the inherent risk of the site itself.

PREPARATION

This is a board game, so you will need a pair of dice and small things to use as counters. You will also need to prepare a 'game-board' – essentially a piece of paper with a table printed on it that identifies a series of potential risks at a heritage site. If everyone works at one particular site, use it to fill in the sheet.

Here is an example for a castle, but it can be adapted for a historic ship, railway, canal or country park or indeed any other historic place that welcomes visitors.

START HERE →	steep stairs in the castle	a glass case containing objects	the site car park	soggy grass	
	the shop	only one member of staff on duty	a long walk to the next part of the site	a very wet day	
	a high walkway	a very hot day	builders on site	a theatre performance on site	
	a cobbled surface	a steep drop with no handrail	a river next to the site	a soft play area for children	
	the tea room	the front door to the site	the site toilets	a garden with historic plants in it	END HERE →

WHAT TO DO

Ask people to list six different ways people behave at heritage sites that can contribute to risks. These need not be 'poor' behaviour – it can just be how people naturally are. For example, you might identify:

1. Unaccompanied children
2. People with impaired mobility
3. Large groups of people
4. Poor visibility (e.g. low light or evening visits)
5. Taking photographs (e.g. selfies)
6. Wanting to touch things/climb things

Write the six behaviours up on the board at the front of the room, then explain the rules to the players:

> *You have a pair of dice. When it is your turn, roll the first dice to determine your place on the board.*
>
> *Next, roll the second dice to get a behaviour from the list on the board. Using the example above, if you roll a 4, the behaviour is 'poor visibility'.*
>
> *You must now identify a risk for the site feature you have landed on, based on that behaviour. For example: 'a glass case' plus 'low visibility' = visitors might knock themselves on the edge of the case. Or 'only one member of staff on duty' plus 'wanting to climb things' = children could easily climb up onto dangerous masonry unnoticed.*

There may be some options where you can't identify risks and that is fine. End the game when people have done at least one run through of the board game, but if there is time, go around the board a couple of times.

DISCUSSION

Explore the ways in which 'risk' at a heritage site is a combination of the inherent risks of a site (e.g. a long drop or a trip hazard) and human behaviour (how people use and access the site). Risk assessment also involves balancing the severity of the incident with the likelihood that it might happen. For example, you could have a part of the site that is really dangerous (such as a long drop) but because it is high and hard to access, relatively few visitors go there. The consequences of a fall are very serious but the likelihood may be small. Alternatively you may have a minor trip hazard near the front door, where almost every visitor goes. The consequences of a trip may be less, but the likelihood of it happening is much higher.

7.4 DO THE PAPERWORK –
WRITE A HEALTH AND SAFETY RISK ASSESSMENT

Written risk assessments are now a core part of site management. Different jurisdictions have different formal requirements for how to do this, but the general principles are the same: think about the ways in which your event or site might be risky; think about the likelihood or severity of that risk; find ways to mitigate that risk. If you can, do this activity after you have done the role play scenario that was set out earlier in this section.

AIM

To become familiar with the process of writing a risk assessment for a heritage site that is open to visitors.

PREPARATION

This is best done at a heritage site or museum. You will need to prepare copies of a standard risk assessment template for each team. The template identifies the risk, the likelihood of the risk and then multiplies likelihood by severity in order to get the risk score. The final column identifies how the risk can be mitigated or reduced/avoided. An example is given in the first row.

Risk	Likelihood 1–5	Severity 1–5	L x S	Mitigation
Identify a risk that might arise from the way someone behaves at a particular place	How likely is it to happen from 1–5 where 1 is not very likely	If it happens, how severe would it be where 1 is not very severe		What action can you take to reduce the likelihood or severity of the risk?
Example: A visitor might slip on wet grass	*2*	*2*	*4*	*Additional signage on wet days or speak to visitors as they enter*

WHAT TO DO

Explain that:

> *You have a new job as a health and safety inspector for the museum/heritage site. Your job is to provide the museum/site director with a health and safety risk assessment. Find a part of the heritage site that might potentially present a health and safety risk. Think about (or observe) the types of visitors, visitor behaviour and working practices of staff around that part of the site.*

Ask people to work in pairs with notebooks or cameras. Suggest they choose a specific area such as the staircase, the front desk, an area of grass, a store, some chairs. Fill in the risk assessment worksheet either on site or back at the classroom using the notes they made on site.

DISCUSSION

Ask each team to discuss one or more of the risks that they looked at and how they mitigated them. For people in the group who happen to work at or are responsible for the site, has this exercise changed the way they operate? Or is it simply a way of setting down what they are already doing to mitigate risk?

⚜ 7.5 ROOFS, GUTTERS AND DOWNPIPES – MAINTENANCE FOR BEGINNERS

Whether you manage a gallery, museum or heritage attraction that is open to the public, or care for a church or other old building, or simply live in an old house with a big garden, you will be very aware of the consequences of ignoring day-to-day maintenance, land care or housekeeping. This activity is designed to introduce people who are not specialists to maintenance planning. I have based it on the example of a historic site, but you can adapt it to other kinds of heritage, such as boats, locomotives, historic aircraft or indeed collections. If you do so, think of a different title for this exercise – for example a conservator training a group of volunteers to care for historic paintings might call the exercise 'Dings, Dust and Damp – Collections Care for Beginners'.

⁞⁞ AIM

To begin to see and be aware of basic maintenance tasks for a museum, gallery, building or heritage asset, including its collections items.

⁞⁞ PREPARATION

You will need to do this activity on site. You will also need a classroom space, ideally with a large table. Give each team ten cards. Notebooks or phone cameras are useful.

⁞⁞ WHAT TO DO

You are the new expert consultant. You may be a conservator, architect, surveyor, curator, landscape manager or ecologist.

The boss has asked you to undertake a very rapid survey to identify the current maintenance issues at the site.

As you are a very expensive expert consultant, she can only afford to pay for 20 minutes of your time.

But because you need to justify your fee, you will need to identify ten maintenance issues in that time and note each one on a card.

The time constraint will help keep up the energy on site. The requirement to identify ten issues is designed to ensure that people go beyond the more obvious issues. After 20 minutes, blow a whistle to stop the exercise.

⠿ DISCUSSION

Back in the classroom, spread out all the cards on a large table. Work in teams if necessary. Ask the participants to sort the cards into the type of maintenance issues they encountered. For a building, the issues might be to do with roofs, gutters and downpipes, finishes, vegetation etc. For items in a collection, the issues might be damage from mould, poor climate control or lighting.

⠿

VARIATION

Once you have identified the top maintenance issues, you could go on to develop a maintenance plan. Provide people with a worksheet containing the core headings for a maintenance plan and ask them to fill it in, using their own observations.

Issue	Remedial action	Frequency	Who?
Example: Peeling paint on window sills	*Rub down and repaint*	*About every 2–3 years?*	*Can be done by local volunteers*

7.6 WHAT DATE SHOULD WE RESTORE IT TO? HERITAGE RECIPES AND BEYOND

One of the questions most often asked by people who are not directly involved in heritage is: 'How do you decide what period to restore something to?' to which my response is invariably, 'It depends on what is important!' Questions of restoration come up over and over again, whether in relation to the conservation of landscapes, buildings or objects, or for other heritage items such as boats, cars or machinery. I prefer to use the heritage impact process in Section 5 as a guide because restoration is just another form of new work, and exactly the same principles apply. However, if you do want to address the restoration issue head on, this activity is a variation that can be played on site or in a classroom. It explores the classic heritage 'recipes' or 'r' words – repair, restoration, reinstatement, replication, recording, etc. – plus a few extra. My personal view is that a values-based approach makes them redundant as primary drivers for decision-making. Perhaps you could ask your group to decide!

Another variation encourages a group to take an audience-based approach to the traditional heritage recipes. We are used to thinking about audiences in interpretation projects, but rarely do so in relation to conservation, as it is usually seen as a purely technical issue. This activity challenges that.

AIM

To introduce concepts such as restoration, and debate how they might be used.

PREPARATION

Pick a 'Major Monument'. If you're playing this in a classroom, it could be something like Stonehenge in the UK (or another well-known site in your country). If you're playing this on site, pick something that is in poor condition – it might be something like a locomotive or ship, or an area of collapsed masonry – and designate it a 'Major Monument' for the purposes of the exercise.

Write each of the following onto a large piece of cardboard, and then cut it up to make twelve individual cards.

Repair	Restore to an earlier period	Reinstate lost features or items	Replicate/Re-create
Record and allow to decay	Revive with something brand new	Repatriate – return it to traditional owners	Retain it as a ruin
Re-use or re-occupy	Remove everything after a certain date	Re-imagine it	Retreat – do nothing

WHAT TO DO

Explain that:

> You are the head of a heritage consultancy firm. The director of [English Heritage/local heritage service/the city] has asked you to come up with a whole new approach to managing this major monument.

Divide people into small teams, and ask each team to pick a card at random. Then ask them to come up with a strategy based on the card.

For Stonehenge, you might restore it to its original appearance or return it to local Pagans, or simply do nothing. Each team has to be able to argue strongly for the approach that is on the card that they have chosen.

Encourage as much creativity as possible. Even the 'Do nothing' option can be fun, as you might argue to spend the money on activities rather than the site. Encourage people to find interesting ways to present their arguments, such as a drawing.

Once teams have finalized their ideas, they will need to present them. Before you begin the presentations, explain that:

> All of you are also members of a funding body. You are a formal panel who must vote on which proposal you will fund. You must abstain from voting for your own project.

Conduct a formal panel with presentations from each team. Ask everyone to deliberate and vote on which project should be funded.

⋮⋮ DISCUSSION

Once the presentations have been voted on, open up the question of how the panel decided and on what basis. In particular, probe the way in which values come into the decision. Is there a right approach for the monument? If not, how do you decide?

⁙

VARIATION

This time you are not a funding panel. Instead, the aim is to explain your strategy for the monument to a particular audience.

Create a second series of cards nominating characters. Ask teams to pick both a strategy card and a character. The aim is to come up with a strategy and to be able to explain it to the character you have chosen.

An eminent Italian conservator	Torvald, the cool Danish design thinker	Bill Smith, the London cabbie	Mary Jenkins, the civil engineer
Carwyn Evans, the local business owner	Tavi Horton, a creative young museum interpreter	Yusuf Muhammed, a local teenager	Your grandmother
Auntie Patricia, a clan elder and traditional owner	A born-digital 15 year old (any culture!)	The local mayor	Trevor Molyneux, the local historic buildings expert

For example, 'Explain to Mary Jenkins the civil engineer why doing nothing to the monument is a good idea' or 'Explain to your grandmother why your creative re-imagining is a good idea'.

Ask people to present their strategies.

⋮⋮ *Discussion*

After the presentations, open up a discussion about conservation and audiences. We often think about interpretation in terms of audience engagement but not conservation. Yet if we are in receipt of public funding to do work and the work will affect what is important to people, we need to consider how different people perceive the value of what we do. For example, the debate around issues such as re-wilding in nature, or the repair of major monuments or buildings damaged in fire or other disasters, inevitably have a political and social dimension as well as a technical one.

♣ 7.7 PROJECT MANAGEMENT 'SNAKES AND LADDERS'

Project management is a vital part of any heritage organization or management activity – from major construction projects to smaller projects such as planning an activity day. This activity is useful for a group of volunteers who may need to hone their skills in project planning.

▓ *AIM*

To illustrate the importance of project management in heritage.

▓ *PREPARATION*

You will need a very large sheet of paper for each team, some counters and a set of dice (one for each team).

▓ *WHAT TO DO*

Ask people to get into teams of no more than four people. Each team will create a project management 'Snakes and Ladders' board game. They must first begin by identifying a heritage 'project'. It might be:

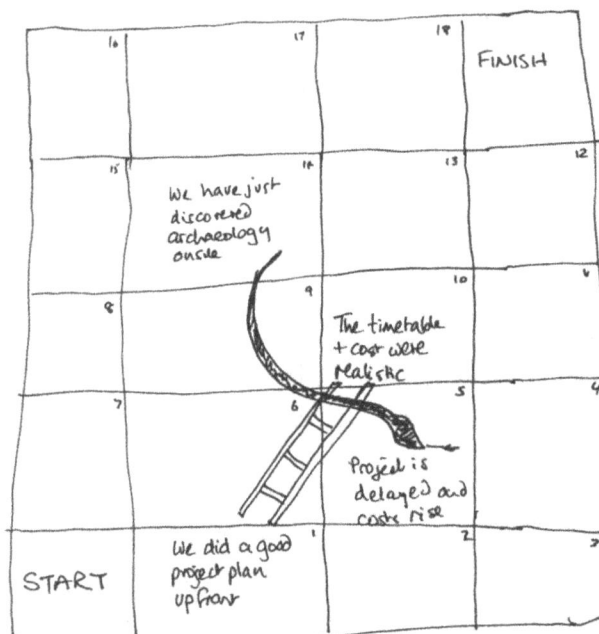

- creating a new children's playground in a historic park
- organizing a visit to the museum for elderly people from a care home
- developing a new policy on managing heritage buildings for lots of different stakeholders
- getting a historic waterwheel working again

For the board game, ask each team to:

> *Make a list of at least five things that might cause the project to go well and five things that might cause it to fail or go badly. On the large piece of paper, draw a grid of twenty squares. Number each square starting at the bottom left and ending at the top right.*

> *Now draw in five descending snakes and five ladders. Write one of the five things that could go well in the square at the bottom of each 'ladder' and something that might cause it to fail in the square at the tail of each 'snake'. Invent consequences at the other end of each, e.g. 'your project has been approved – advance three squares'.*

When teams have finished designing their board, they can pass it on to the next team to play the game: each player will have a counter and will throw the dice to work out how many squares to advance. If a player hits the tail of a snake, they must go sliding down to the 'head'. If a player lands on the bottom of a ladder, they can climb up to the top.

⠿ DISCUSSION

Open up a discussion about the value of good project management and the relevance of project management thinking to participants' own roles. If people in your group are working on a real project, you can then go on to help them with other basic project-related skills like options appraisal, developing a business plan and a timeline.

7.8 WHEN EXPERTS COLLIDE 2 – GUESS THE HERITAGE SPECIALIST!

Most heritage sites involve more than one kind of heritage, requiring people with different specialist backgrounds to work together. For example, a museum might be responsible for an area of park, for large items of engineering heritage or for historic buildings, as well as their collections. This activity is designed for a group of people working in heritage who come from different backgrounds.

AIM

To improve cross-disciplinary working in cultural heritage by exploring the ways people with different expertise, knowledge or professional backgrounds approach heritage.

PREPARATION

You will need a case study that involves a proposal to do something major at an important heritage site. For example, the proposal could be to build a new visitor centre in the grounds of a cathedral or castle.

WHAT TO DO

Ask everyone to organize themselves into pairs or teams according to their skills, professional background or area of interest. For example:

- architects or people with a building background
- archaeologists or historians or people with a research background
- ecologists or biologists or those who deal with natural heritage
- people who are part of a community group
- people with corporate skills, such as HR, finance etc.
- commercial experts, such as people with skills in business development, marketing, venue hire etc.

If you don't have people with the same background in the room, simply ask people to work with those whose background is closest to theirs.

Ask the teams to:

Spend a few minutes thinking about the proposal. What are the top priorities for your specialist area in order to get the project moving?

For example, archaeologist might want to make sure the fabric of the site is properly understood before any changes are made, whilst the commercial team will want to make sure that there is a sound business plan.

> *For your team – what makes a good heritage project? And what is your profession's preferred working style (detail or big picture, words or pictures)? What is your profession really good at? What does your profession tend to be less good at? Answer these four questions on a big sheet of flip-chart paper. Do not identify your team on the sheet.*

Put each sheet up on the wall or board at the front. Ask everyone if they can identify which team was responsible for which sheet.

DISCUSSION

Talk about the similarities and differences and preferred working styles for each specialist area. Take it a step further and look at where conflicts may arise and how to avoid them.

VARIATION

A simpler version of the game is to show an image of a heritage item. Ask each team to write an anonymous description of it from their perspective using no more than 100 words. Put each sheet on the wall and see if people can identify which team wrote which description.

✹ 7.9 SHOPPING SAFARI – WHAT CAN THE MALL TEACH US ABOUT SITE PRESENTATION?

For heritage sites that are open to the public as visitor attractions, site presentation matters hugely in terms of messages, customer service and how your visitors see you. It is also one of those things that you only notice when it is done badly. Presentation is about all the values displayed through everything that you or your organization does in relation to a heritage asset or place (as opposed to the core significance of the heritage asset itself). It can include things such as whether you allow vehicles on a heritage site during opening hours, how staff welcome visitors, how rooms in a historic house are dressed, or the design of signage and information. This activity involves a trip to a shopping mall and also a visit to a heritage site. To make the best use of time, you could combine it with the next activity, 'Retail Therapy'. A variation on the activity makes more use of the five senses in shaping perceptions on a site. You can also think about how different audiences might react to the way the site is presented.

⁛ AIM

To introduce the concept of site presentation.

⁛ PREPARATION

This activity should ideally start with a trip to a local shopping mall followed by a trip to a heritage site to compare approaches. It can still be played if you only have the time, resources (or access) to one or the other. You will need clipboards and photocopies of the Site Presentation Checklist (or tablets and downloads). The Site Presentation Checklist is as follows:

The 10 Ss of Site Presentation	Shopping Mall	Museum or Heritage Site
Starters – what are your first impressions of the site?		
Staff – how do they greet you?		
Site – is it clean and tidy?		
Signage – can you find your way around? Can you find what you need?		
Safety – do you feel safe and comfortable?		
Security – is it necessary? Is it obtrusive or unobtrusive?		
Sense – what can you hear, see, smell, taste or touch? what impression does it leave		
Sense of place – what kind of place are you in? How does it make you feel? What is the quality of the experience?		
Sincerity (or authenticity) – is the place true to its origins and messages? Does it have a clear identity or brand?		
Sign-off – what are your last impressions as you leave the site?		

❦ WHAT TO DO

Start at the shopping mall. Give everyone a copy of the Site Presentation Checklist and ask them to fill it out on site in pairs or teams. To keep things moving and ensure that people focus on first impressions, give them a strict time limit – perhaps 15–20 minutes and no more. Once that is complete, visit the heritage site and fill in a second copy of the Site Presentation Checklist.

❦ DISCUSSION

When you come back to the classroom, compare and contrast the two experiences. Does the heritage site or museum have anything to learn from the shopping mall? Does the shopping mall have anything to learn from the heritage site?

What can the mall teach us about retailing at heritage sites? Are there any lessons on presentation more generally? How is the mall encouraging people to make choices? What kinds of values are they tapping into? Think about visual aesthetics and attractiveness.

Ironically, many heritage sites such as fortifications or castles were historically designed to keep people out – yet today the aim is to attract and welcome visitors. How can this be resolved using lessons from shopping experiences?

VARIATION

People use all of their senses at heritage sites. The checklist above mentions different senses in passing, but another variation is to spend more time on site focusing on those senses.

At either the shopping mall or the heritage site, ask each person to work through the senses in turn. What can they see? What can they hear? What can they taste? And what can they smell?

Back together again, talk about the different sensory perceptions of the site. Organize the answers under each of the senses.

If you have a big group, you can vary the exercise by asking different teams to fill in the form from the perspective of a different character (or audience) – e.g. an 18 year old, a mother with a toddler, a group of experts, or a family on holiday who don't speak the local language.

⁜ 7.10 RETAIL THERAPY – VISUAL MERCHANDISING BINGO

Retailing plays a critical role in most museums and heritage sites that are open to the public as visitor attractions. However, the reality is that, unlike straightforward commercial environments, retailing at visitor attractions is both a way of generating income and a core part of the visitor experience. Indeed, for some high-volume museums and sites, the retailing experience can be more popular than the museum itself. On the other hand, many smaller sites don't have the footfall or turnover to justify a retail outlet or staffing, but visitors expect to be able to buy a memento of some sort, hence the need to recognize it as part of the visitor experience as much as a commercial activity.

Understanding what matters about heritage and why is as important to retailing as it is to any other aspect of managing heritage visitor attractions. Visual merchandising is the activity that involves developing spaces, floor plans and displays with the aim of attracting, engaging and motivating the visitor to buy something that may provide a tangible object as a reminder and possibly extend/deepen the experience of the visit. Specialist museum visual merchandiser Arantxa Garcia says, 'my favourite shops are those that are true to their collections'[1] – in other words those that reflect the value and significance of the collections.

Just as a visit to the local shopping mall was a good start for thinking about site presentation, it is also a useful start for thinking about retailing and visual merchandising. Whilst you are at the shopping mall, think about retail in more depth. If doing two activities is confusing or unwieldy, appoint one team as the Visual Merchandising Team and ask them to focus on retail sales, and the others as the Presentation Team, who will focus on the overall presentation of the mall.

⁜ AIM

To introduce the basic concepts of visual merchandising.

⁜ PREPARATION

Prepare copies of the Visual Merchandising Bingo worksheet. The following is based on common visual merchandising themes, but you can adapt it to your own requirements.

---

1. Arantxa Garcia, 'What's the Creative Process in Visual Merchandising?', British Library blog, 12 August 2014, http://britishlibrary.typepad.co.uk/inspiredby/2014/08/whats-the-creative-process-in-visual-merchandising-arantxa-garcia-on-comics-unmasked.html.

The power of three Merchandise organized in threes to provide symmetry	Like with like Goods grouped together to show the depth of a range	Outside in A clean clear window with a good story to tell	Strike zone A gondola just inside the store with a good range of merchandise
The pyramid principle Grouping items from high to low	You know who A shop with a very clear target audience	Right hand down Use of the inside wall on the right for premium products	You know you want it Impulse items just tempting you to buy
Product placement Sale items at the back of the store to draw you in	Colour counts Good use of colour to reinforce a brand or product range	Draw me in A well-located point of sale	Loud and clear An example of a clear signage strategy with matching art, font, colours and message
Show don't tell An example of goods displayed so that the customer can see how they would look at home	Dark to light Darker items lower down and brighter ones higher up	Shine a light A good example of one of the following: general lighting, accent lighting and task lighting	Progression Items arranged in a sequence – small to large, left to right
Action stations Witty, attention-grabbing props	Cross-mix product A mixture of products with a similar theme	Right to the edge An example of a positive impact using the walls of a store	Great gondolas or fab fixtures Example of high-quality shop fittings

⠿ WHAT TO DO

Visit the mall, and see if you can find an example of each of the visual merchandising techniques set out in the Visual Merchandising Bingo worksheet. Note the example on the sheet, or take a photo of each if the retailer is content.

The exercise finishes when the team has found one of each (or after a fixed time – perhaps an hour). Offer additional points if the teams can find more than one in a single store.

⁞⁞ *DISCUSSION*

Have a general discussion about visual merchandising – why does it matter? What difference does it make?

If you are working with a specific museum or visitor attraction, explore issues such as:

- What lessons can be applied to the site?
- What differences are there?
- Is the aesthetic and approach of a retail mall right for the visitor attraction?
- How might you develop a visual merchandising approach for the attraction?
- How might the values of the site or collection influence that strategy?

7.11 CREATE A PRODUCT RANGE THAT REFLECTS HERITAGE VALUE

AIM

To introduce the idea of product ranges and how they might reflect the distinctive nature of the museum or heritage visitor attraction.

PREPARATION

Either play this on site or use a case study that you have prepared in advance. The information for the case study should provide participants with basic information about a museum or heritage visitor attraction and should include:

- what it is,
- why it is important,
- what the annual visitor numbers are and,
- any further information about the visitor profile.

You will need large pieces of paper and coloured pens.

WHAT TO DO

Introduce the case study. Tell each team:

> *You have been appointed to the role of retail buyer for a new shop at this heritage visitor attraction. You have been asked to develop a suite of ten products that best capture the spirit of the place and that will also make a healthy return.*

Ask each team to draw or describe on a piece of paper each of their products, and set them out as a 'shop'.

DISCUSSION

Will the other teams buy their products? Are they happy customers? Does the product range enhance the experience of the heritage asset? If so, how?

⁂ 7.12 BETWEEN A ROCK AND A HARD PLACE – HERITAGE LEADERSHIP FOR BEGINNERS

I devised this activity for a staff away day – the topic I was given was 'leadership', but this seems best to encapsulate what much day-to-day leadership involves, especially in public sector organizations. It is similar to the 'Consequences' game that I played as a child, in that you write things on a sheet of paper and pass it on. You don't need to fold the paper over though!

⁞⁞· *AIM*

To develop skills in dealing with everyday problems at heritage sites.

⁞⁞· *PREPARATION*

This activity is done in teams – you will just need large sheets of paper and pens.

⁞⁞· *WHAT TO DO*

In brief, each team writes something on a sheet of paper and passes it to the next team.

Step One

Ask each team to pick a public heritage site or museum. Write the name on the top of a large sheet of paper and pass the sheet to the next team.

Step Two

Now ask the next team to come up with a really great idea for the site or gallery or place – it could be interpretation, new build, a wildly creative installation or just something that would be really wonderful to do. Write down the idea on the sheet of paper, leaving plenty of space below it, and pass it on to the next team.

Step Three

The next step is to think of three very good reasons why the idea cannot be implemented. They should be realistic and based on experience – for example,

- there is no budget for events
- the neighbours will object to the noise
- fireworks are dangerous

Pass the paper to the next team.

Step Four

This is the main part of the activity. The job of each team is to find a way to implement the great idea, having been given the reasons why it may not happen. Think of a creative plan to deal with the issues – or to slightly tweak the idea so that it can happen!

⁞⁝· *DISCUSSION*

Present the ideas to the whole group. Give small prizes for the best and cleverest work! You will find that the issue of values has come up in and around how people deal with obstacles – often understanding what is really important is the key to then deciding how best to deal with them.

8

❖

VALUES IN HERITAGE POLICY, EVALUATION AND ADVOCACY

People who work in museums and heritage constantly need to make the case for the benefits of what they do. Whether it is to a politician, a funding agency, project partners or the public, it is vital to find ways to explain how and why caring for heritage matters.

The reason this is so hard is that the financial return on investment is not usually an adequate measure of the value of heritage. Put simplistically, in the private sector, organizations create value by generating income for shareholders and others through providing goods and services. In the public or not-for-profit sector, the measure of value is more complex and cannot simply be measured in terms of money (although there are lots of economic techniques that aim to do just that).

The question of how to capture or measure the wider value of investing in heritage is not new – environmental economists pioneered thinking about how to apply economic models of value to environmental outcomes. In other sectors such as health and the arts, there has also been a lot of work to capture the value of investment in creative outcomes, and there is now a growing body of literature on the value of caring for heritage.

The activities in this section focus on ways to articulate the wider benefits of investing in heritage. They are designed for volunteer or community groups who advocate for heritage, or for people involved in heritage policy or leadership.

⬡ 8.1 STARTER – WHAT IF THERE WERE NO HERITAGE?

Often the value of heritage only becomes apparent to decision-makers when it is under threat, or lost following a disaster or conflict. This activity is similar to 1.7, 'The Meaning of Lost Places', but the focus here is on drawing out the implications for policy and advocacy.

⠿ AIM

To explore the role of loss or threat in reminding people of the value of heritage and to think about the implications of this for heritage policy today and in the future.

⠿ WHAT TO DO

Ask the group:

> *What if there were no heritage?*
>
> *Describe your village, town or city without its heritage? What would be missing?*
>
> *Think about your life if there were no heritage. What would it be like? What would you most miss?*

Ask the group to find creative ways to respond – perhaps with a drawing . . .

> *Has focussing on loss changed your perceptions of your own heritage? And if so, does this also happen with wider communities and their perceptions of heritage?*

⠿ DISCUSSION

Use these personal perceptions of loss and the fact that heritage is often something that we only value once it has disappeared to discuss the wider implications for policy-making. For example, it can be difficult to find resources to maintain a heritage asset unless there is a major fire or other disaster. Drawing on your own knowledge and that of the group, talk about specific examples of where major risks to heritage assets have led to new investment or stronger policies. How has this shaped heritage policy and practice over the years?

❦ 8.2 THE PUBLIC VALUE OF HERITAGE – 'SIGNIFICANCE', SUSTAINABILITY AND SERVICE

This activity illustrates the 'Public Value' model for heritage, which brings together the three different ways in which caring for heritage can create value, and it helps to explain the difference between the value and significance of a heritage item and other kinds of values. It is a simple and powerful way of exploring heritage values. I use it as a teaching activity after delivering the activities in Section 3, 'The Big Picture', or to help a group think about how to evaluate a heritage project.

Please note that 'significance' in this activity is used as a shorthand term for the values that define heritage assets.

⠿ *AIM*

To introduce the idea of public value in heritage and to identify different kinds of value that an organization can create in order to demonstrate it.

⠿ *PREPARATION*

You will need a hat or bowl, a whiteboard, some small pieces of paper and felt-tip pens, as well as some larger Post-It notes. The facilitator should be familiar with the three kinds of value that form part of the 'Public Value' model for heritage.

⠿ *WHAT TO DO*

Start by asking:

> *How much money is spent on heritage in your country or organization?*

The figure might be the budget of the museum, or even how much the government puts towards museums and all other heritage activities. In the UK, the National Lottery Heritage Fund has spent around £7 billion on heritage. The figure does not have to be exact or accurate. Write the number in very large letters on the whiteboard. Ask:

> *Who is going to care about that money and how it is spent?*

Write down each answer on a slip of paper; for example, it might be 'politicians', 'the media', 'ticket buyers', 'heritage specialists' or 'local communities'. Put the slips of paper into a hat and ask each team to pick one. Ask teams to spend a few minutes identifying what the people they have picked might care about.

⁝⁞· *DISCUSSION*

Go round each team in turn, asking them to explain what might be most important to their group. Divide the responses into three groups to reflect the three different points of the 'Public Value of Heritage' triangle:

- **Significance** – caring for and protecting what matters to people (intrinsic values).
- **Sustainability** – the economic, environmental and community values that might flow from investment in heritage (instrumental benefits).
- **Service** – issues such as trust, transparency, accountability and fairness, as well as the service offered to the public – great experiences, fantastic customer service, a great welcome (institutional values).

Not all of the feedback will fit neatly into one of these categories – I put comments about heritage under 'Significance', comments about wider benefits to local places, jobs, etc. under 'Sustainability' and points about transparency, accountability and organizational behaviour under 'Service'. As you do this, explain the different kinds of value, drawing on observations that the group have made. You could also talk about which topics have come up over and over again. If institutional values such as trust and accountability come up more often than traditional heritage values such as significance – ask the group what this might mean for heritage organizations.

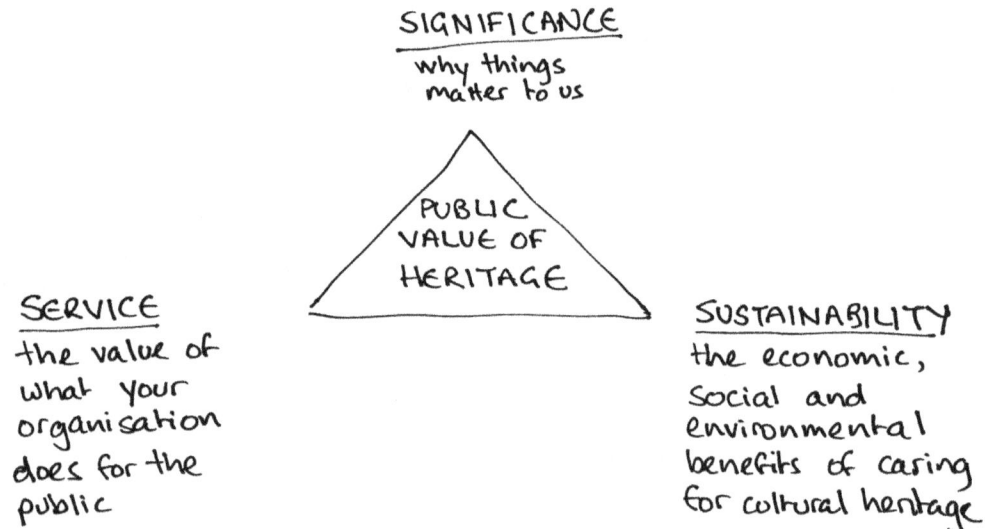

❦ 8.3 ONLY CONNECT –
WHAT CAN HERITAGE DO FOR YOU?

People who volunteer or work with heritage are very used to *that* dinner party conversation – the one where the person next to you finds out what you do, looks very superior and turns politely away to talk to the person on the other side. It is hard for people to overcome the assumption that heritage enthusiasts are 'backward looking' and unconnected to the real world.

One of the challenges for cultural and heritage organizations is to make the link between heritage and other agendas – such as the economy, society and the environment. Too often, heritage is seen as a luxury rather than something that can play a role in the wider world. This activity is designed to help people make those links and is particularly useful for anyone who works in a government heritage organization or in policy.

⋮⋮ *AIM*

To better understand how caring for cultural heritage can contribute to different areas of life and in public policy.

⋮⋮ *WHAT TO DO*

First ask people to make a list of organizations, people or professions that don't always seem to 'get' heritage. They might be local, state or national government, businesses or professions such a property developers or accountants. For this activity, these are your 'sectors'.

I HATE HERITAGE!

— *MAYOR*

... but the Local council:
- are responsible for parks which include heritage
- look after historic archives
- manage museums
- make planning decisions that affect historic places
- invest in regenerating areas that include historic buildings

Provide each team with a large sheet of paper. Ask people to:

> *Choose one sector. Think about what they do, and make a list of all of the different ways in which they might be involved in cultural heritage as a result.*

For example, they might be involved in heritage as a result of their role in:

- tourism or marketing
- planning or regulating development
- keeping archives or records
- providing incentives such as tax or rates relief, or grants
- owning and managing property (e.g. parks, historic buildings, infrastructure, etc.) that are also heritage

- providing public access to facilities (e.g. libraries, museums, urban parks)
- providing other services such as schools, transport, health or housing

   Now, drawing on that list, write down some of the things that your sector might be able to achieve as a result of their involvement in heritage.

For example, a local council could achieve health outcomes by caring for parks; they could address poverty and social exclusion by supporting libraries; they might attract tourism by helping local heritage attractions or investment through regenerating rundown historic areas.

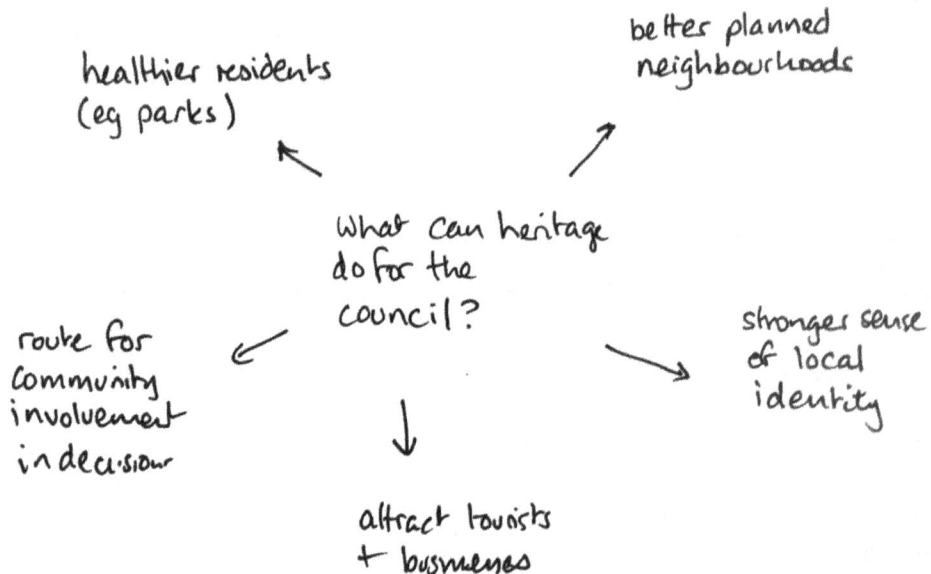

DISCUSSION

Think about the range of benefits that heritage can bring to the agendas of non-heritage specialists or organizations. Then think about what heritage people need to do as part of their own heritage practice to better make those connections!

⚛ 8.4 KILLER FACTS – DO THE NUMBERS

One of the challenges in heritage policy is finding the 'Killer Facts' that help make the case for the value of heritage, or dispel myths about it. A common concern expressed by people who work with heritage is that there is a lack of specific data about the economic, social or environmental impacts of caring for heritage. Whilst this is true, there are often other sources of data that can be called upon to help make the case for the benefits of investing in or looking after heritage assets.

⁑ *AIM*

To identify potential data sets for heritage by starting with an understanding of our own personal engagement with it.

⁑ *WHAT TO DO*

This activity is probably best done in pairs.

> *Think about the past 24 hours and list all of the possible encounters with heritage that you had during this time. Write the list on the left side of the paper.*

This might be via a TV programme or walking home through a historic street. There could be a direct encounter or an indirect one (e.g. 'my daughter learned about the Second World War yesterday').

My house is more than 100 years old…

I wonder how many other people live in older houses?

> *For each encounter you have identified, think of a data set that you could use to get some measure of how many other people might have done something similar.*

Encounter	Potential Data Set
Example: I live in an old house	*How much of the national housing stock is over fifty years old?*

⠏· *DISCUSSION*

Discuss the range of data that can be collected to evaluate heritage. Which of these are the 'Killer Facts', i.e. the figures that are most convincing and which have the potential to change people's assumptions? If the group is all part of one organization, make a list of the top 'facts' that you could use to make the case for what they do. For example, for a museum is it just visitor numbers? What more can the museum deliver? What numbers might help make that case?

♛ 8.5 FIRST STEPS IN EVALUATION

Whatever kind of heritage we work with, we will at some point need to evaluate the success or failure of a project, either because it is a formal requirement of funding or because it is good practice. This activity is a simple starter to introduce the idea of evaluation to a group. If they do then want to go on to undertake or commission a proper evaluation of a project, they can use one of the many existing evaluation toolkits. For a museum or heritage project, a toolkit that includes some consideration of values would be best. How the value of the heritage is defined will affect the success or failure of the project. Without some understanding at the outset of what is considered significant by whom, and how, it is impossible to second guess the success or failure of that project. A toolkit that many heritage projects have used is the New Economics Foundation (NEF) 'Prove it' toolkit, which uses a 'story board' and a theory of change.

⁞⁞ AIM

To introduce the concept of evaluation in heritage projects.

⁞⁞ WHAT TO DO

Tell everyone that:

> *You are members of the board of a heritage funding organization. You have £50,000 to commission a heritage group to do a project.*

Either suggest projects or ask for suggestions. For example, the money might be used to fund a community group to record wildlife, research a site, build a website, repair a historic church, support an archives advisor in a local council or develop an education programme for a museum. Put the group into teams and explain the following:

> *You will have to report back to the chair of your board on what the project achieved and whether it was good value for money. List the information you will require.*

While they are working, write a list of questions on the board:

- How will you know if the project has succeeded?
- What difference will the project make?
- What information do you want the project to collect?
- How should it be collected?
- How should it be presented?

As the teams feed back, look at whether they have addressed each of these issues in their list of information required.

⠿ DISCUSSION

Explore the similarities and differences in the lists that teams have created. Can you create a single evaluation process on the board from what people have said? You could take the discussion a step further by asking how the requirements would change if the organization were to receive £10,000? What about £100,000? Is evaluation a good use of money? If not, why not? If so, how much is appropriate to spend on evaluation?

⁙ 8.6 HOW'S OUR DRIVING? EVALUATING OUTCOMES USING 'COMMEMORATIVE INTEGRITY'

We don't often stop to ask how well we are doing. One of the few organizations to do this consistently is Parks Canada, who have a toolkit called Commemorative Integrity for their public monuments.

⠇⠄ *AIM*

To use the Parks Canada 'Commemorative Integrity' toolkit to evaluate how well an agency or group are looking after their heritage asset or site that is open to the public.

⠇⠄ *PREPARATION*

Although originally designed for historic sites, Commemorative Integrity could also be used for other types of heritage such as a collection, landscape or piece of machinery. You will need to be able to visit the site, but you will also need access to a quiet workspace. In advance of the day, obtain copies of any formal heritage protection documents for the site such as the listing description or the statement of outstanding universal value, and also a copy the Commemorative Integrity Worksheet for each team.

Commemorative Integrity Attribute	Comments
Are the resources directly related to the reasons for the site's designation (e.g. national historic site) impaired or under threat?	
Are the reasons for the site's designation (as a national historic site) effectively communicated to the public?	
Are the site's values respected in all decisions and actions affecting the site?	

⠏ *WHAT TO DO*

Start in the classroom or in a quiet work space. Explain that:

> *You have been appointed to the prestigious role of inspector of monuments [or the new head of collections at the museum etc.]. Your job is to decide how well the site [or museum/collection] is being cared for.*

Allow time for people to read through the documentation. Talk through the criteria for Commemorative Integrity listed on the worksheet and then send the groups out to the site to assess the extent to which the site meets the criteria.

⠏ *DISCUSSION*

When the group returns, ask for their feedback. How well do they think the site is doing against the criteria on the Commemorative Integrity worksheet? If there are issues, what are they? How easy was it to use the criteria? Are the criteria an effective measure of the 'quality' of heritage preservation? Are there other criteria that could be used? Was it possible to assess Commemorative Integrity on the basis of existing information, or would the group want to do further research or interviews?

You could also have an interesting discussion about the extent to which interpretation strategies should reflect the reasons for the site (or collection's) designation or not. Does it matter whether or not visitors are given information about why the site is protected? Or is this irrelevant to creating a great interpretation strategy?

VARIATION

Rather than providing the worksheet and model, ask your audience to come up with their own framework or worksheet to measure how 'well' the organization is doing.

8.7 TACKLING MYTHS HEAD-ON – ALL THE BAD THINGS YOU EVER HEARD ABOUT HERITAGE

A short version of this activity was included as one of the exercises in Section 3, 'The Big Picture'. But for anyone involved in advocacy or policy development for cultural heritage, it is an activity that is worth spending some more time on.

The starting point for this activity is that rather than ignoring negative attitudes to heritage and museums, we need to better understand them – what they are, where they come from and whether or not they are true. Understanding these assumptions and views is a great starting point for thinking about data, advocacy, research and communications strategies.

AIM

To confront negative views of museums and heritage head-on as a starting point for thinking about how to respond to them.

WHAT TO DO

Either as a whole group or in teams, get people to brainstorm every negative statement about heritage or museums they have ever heard. This might include statements such as:

- museums are a luxury we can't afford
- heritage causes delays in planning
- there is no point in keeping old heritage skills such as wooden boatbuilding
- old buildings are more expensive to fix than modern buildings

If you get very general statements, such as 'heritage stops progress' try to turn them into something more specific.

Once you have a list, give one statement to each team and ask them to answer the following questions in relation to that statement (write the questions on the board):

1. Who might (or did) say it?
2. Why might they say it?
3. Is it true?
4. If not why not?
5. What could we do to either counteract it (if not true) or deal with it (if true)?

Talk through the responses. Focus particularly on responses to the question of whether it is true (rarely straightforward) and then the two questions at the end.

:::· *DISCUSSION*

Having been through the exercise, finish by asking people whether it has changed their perceptions at all. If you want to push it a little further, ask for one thing they might do differently as a result of the exercise.

⚇ 8.8 CLOSER – TWO MINUTES IN THE LIFT WITH THE MAYOR

This is the kind of activity to play at the end of a workshop on heritage values. It summarizes everything you have done for the day. Use it for a particular site or project, or to make the case for heritage in general.

⦂⦂ *AIM*

To explain very briefly why heritage is so important.

⦂⦂ *PREPARATION*

Bell or loud egg timer. Small prizes.

⦂⦂ *WHAT TO DO*

The group has 2 minutes in the lift with the Prime Minister/Mayor/funding body or whoever is important!

Divide people into teams. They should elect a spokesperson and prepare a script. The aim is to explain why heritage matters (or their project or site matters) in no more than 2 minutes. Use the timer! Who was the most convincing?

⦂⦂ *DISCUSSION*

No need for a discussion, but you could award a small prize for the presentation that they judge to be the best.

9

VALUES IN HERITAGE LEADERSHIP

Values have a critical role to play in organizations as well as in relation to things or places. At the heart of any organization in either the public or the private sector is the idea that it brings people together to create something of value. Defining how an organization creates value is key to understanding its central purpose. The 'value proposition' underpins everything from structure and functions to its staffing, and ultimately the brand. Equally, organizations can create value not just through profit but through providing a service that people value.

Understanding the culture and values of an organization is key to managing it well. It can be the basis for activities such as defining the core purpose or the brand. Understanding organizational values can also help underpin the process of managing change, or in working through the process of a merger or restructure. Understanding ethical values can help define expected standards or behaviour.

Some of these activities were initially designed specifically for organizations who look after heritage – these might range from local community groups to government departments to charities or private sector companies. They include museums, parks and wildlife bodies, local societies, industrial heritage groups etc. There is also a much larger number of organizations that look after heritage even if it is not their core purpose. Examples include private sector organizations such as hotel chains or groups who hold and manage a lot of property such as hotel groups, the armed forces, government or local authorities, and also not-for-profit organizations. However, these activities are relevant to any organization where there is a need to articulate the way it creates value.

The activities in this section focus on organizational values. But because an organization is, in a way, a form of intangible heritage – with a history and a culture of its own – and because as with any kind of heritage the biggest challenge is often around managing change, you may find that many of the other exercises in this book can be adapted for organizations.

⚏ 9.1 STARTER – TWENTY QUESTIONS ABOUT YOUR PURPOSE

One of the core issues in any organization is to be clear about its purpose. Here is a game you might have played as a child. It is a way to open up discussion about what an organization is for.

⚏ *AIM*

To explore the purpose of an organization.

⚏ *WHAT TO DO*

The game should be played in a circle. The first person makes a statement about the purpose of the organization and then asks 'why?' before passing it on to the next person. They then make a statement and at the end ask 'why?' to the person beside them. For example:

> **We give money to fix historic buildings.** Why?
>
> Because people can't afford to do it themselves. Why?
>
> Because often those buildings don't have a productive use. Why?
>
> Because technology has moved on in farming. Why?

Other examples of 'starters' might be:

- We have objects in our museum
- I restore historic ships
- We are the government's heritage advisors
- We campaign to save wildlife

It does not have to be perfect or elaborate – just a quick top of the head line.

⚏ *DISCUSSION*

It is almost impossible to get to twenty questions, but five or six might just be possible. Even if the game ends in laughter or phrases such as 'just because' after a few questions, there is a bigger point. It is one thing to say what we do but all together another to be clear about why we do it.

⚏

VARIATION

This could also be played in pairs.

⁙ 9.2 SO WHAT DO WE ACTUALLY DO? KEYWORDS

This is another exercise to help define what an organization does as a first step to thinking about how it creates value. It is used by web developers to structure information on a website. It is based on key words that can be an important organizing framework, not just for a website but for other aspects of what an organization does, including data collection and advocacy. The activity also explores what different audiences might want from an organization. It is designed either for a group from one organization or in relation to an organization that most people in the group know a little about.

⁙ *AIM*

To find and map keywords that define what an organization does.

⁙ *PREPARATION*

You will need a supply of blank cards and pens and ideally a table for each team.

⁙ *WHAT TO DO*

Ask teams to list the different things that their organization does, writing one activity on each card.

They should imagine they are developing the organization's website. Teams must lay out the cards in a hierarchy to show the different things that people might want to find out about it or the things that it does. What things might go on the 'landing page'? What things group together? What kind of information might people want?

⁙ *DISCUSSION*

Discuss the usefulness of the key words that have been used and the way teams have organized them. Can the key words they have used to describe the work of the organization be used for other things, such as to define the structure of the organization? Or to file documents or collect data?

Who did the teams have in mind when they were developing their structure? Were they thinking about clients or users of the service? Investors? Or politicians? Or partners? Would different stakeholders be interested in different things?

⁙ 9.3 PEERS, PARTNERS AND POLITICIANS – MAP YOUR AUTHORIZING ENVIRONMENT

This exercise explores the idea of the 'the authorizing environment'[1] – that is, the various groups that enable an organization to function. For museums and other heritage organizations, they may be politicians, government departments, funders, visitors or users, or the people who deliver activities. Understanding the authorizing environment is an important part of thinking about how an organization creates value because different people value different things. A variation looks at the mechanisms that enable an organization to operate.

⁘ *AIM*

To map a heritage organization's authorizing environment as a starting point for thinking about value.

⁘ *WHAT TO DO*

Start by explaining the idea of the authorizing environment. Perhaps use an example from a non-heritage organization, such as the police. Ask:

> *Who it is that enables the police to operate? Who in effect gives them 'permission' to do what they do? What enables them to function? Where does funding come from? Where do powers come from?*

Give each team an organization. It could be one that people in the room work for or belong to, or draw up a list of organizations that everyone in the room will be familiar with. In the UK, it might be the British Museum or Historic Scotland or the Canal and River Trust; in the US, it might be the Getty, the US National Park Service or the US National Trust. Ask each team to:

> *List all of the people or other organizations who enable your organization to function.*

On a large piece of paper, ask each team to write the four 'Ps' of the authorizing environment – 'Politicians', 'Peers', 'Partners', and the 'Public' as illustrated. Using the list of people and organizations, teams should map the authorizing environment, sorting the list into the four 'Ps'. You might find that 'peers' and 'partners' overlap – I distinguish them by identifying 'peers' as the people who work in the same sector as you do and 'partners' as people in other areas who you may need to work with in order to deliver outcomes.

---

1. M.H. Moore, *Creating Public Value: Strategic Management in Government* (Cambridge: Harvard University Press, 1995).

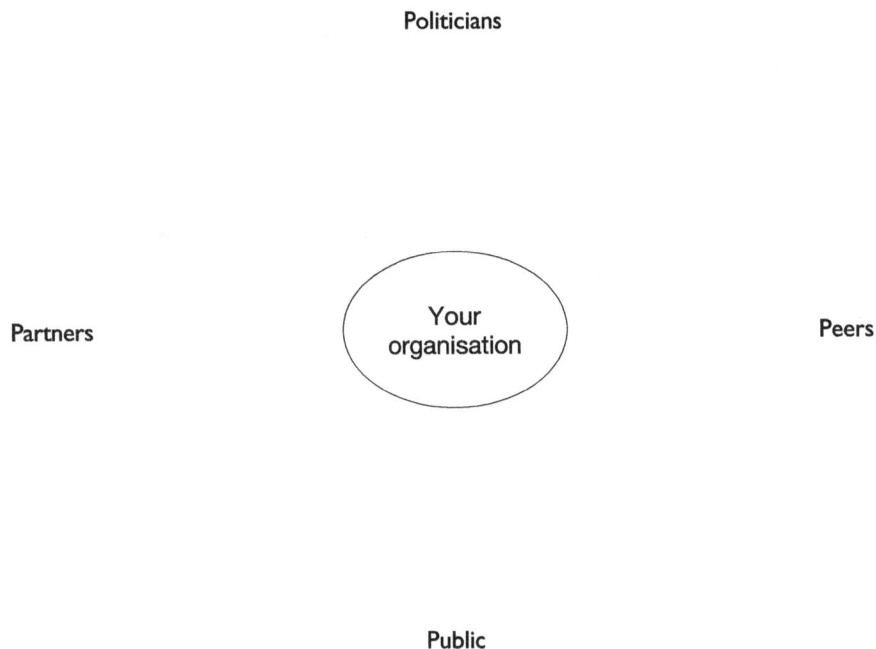

Politicians

Partners

Your organisation

Peers

Public

DISCUSSION

Once each team has mapped their authorizing environment, ask people how they respond to and work with others. Do the four categories work as concepts? Talk about working 'up the line' with politicians and 'down the line' with the public, visitors or customers. Ask how well people work with peers and partners. How can you keep the different groups in balance? Where are people putting most of their effort now? Are they maintaining an equilibrium between all four groups, are they neglecting some? What does each group need? What kind of communication? What kind of information?

VARIATION

As well as mapping the authorizing environment in terms of politicians, peers, partners and the public, you can also map it in terms of mechanisms. This activity is a useful way of helping staff across an organization to understand the wider framework in which the whole organization operates. Ask:

What are the mechanisms that enable your organization to operate?

They will include the legislation or powers under which the organization operates or offers a service; policies that shape the way it works; any charter or constitution that the organization must follow; sources of funding that enable it to operate, which might include grants or donations; they may be the different standards or regulations that you need to comply with (such as health and safety or child protection). They may include structures such as the board, the mandate for the board or the financial reporting system. Include any standards you need to comply with. Ask teams to map these on a piece of paper as a spider diagram. What are the different types of mechanism? Which have the most impact on what the organization does? Where are the biggest risks for the organization? For example, are the risks for a museum bigger in relation to governance or collections conservation?

⠿ 9.3.1 USE THEIR LANGUAGE

One of the biggest challenges in heritage practice is to communicate the contribution that heritage can make to other agendas. One of the barriers is language – we tend to use heritage language rather than the language of other sectors such as business, health or education.

Use the four 'Ps' as a starting point. Pick a heritage achievement – either something your group have achieved themselves or a generic achievement such as a popular exhibition or a great restoration project. Ask each team to name a peer, a partner, a politician and a member of the public and explain that achievement to each, if possible using their language. Keep it very brief and high level.

How did the language and concepts used vary between different groups? What might a politician care about, as opposed to a member of the public or someone in the heritage world?

♥ 9.4 WHAT ARE YOUR BRAND VALUES?

After working with marketing teams, I have learned that there is much in common between developing a statement of significance for a heritage asset and articulating the brand values of an organization. Marketing specialists use an understanding of values as the basis for developing brands and campaigns. This is a traditional marketing game designed to help people think about the character – and by implications values – of their organization. Other activities that can contribute to thinking about brand values include the 'Public Value' activity (8.2) and 'My Best Day Out' (6.8). Section 3, 'The Big Picture', could also be used to articulate the significance of an organization.

AIM

To articulate some of the institutional (or core brand) values for a heritage or cultural organization.

PREPARATION

Make up a series of cards naming general categories. For example:

Car	Animal	Celebrity
Sport	Retail brand	Food
Fashion label	A computer game	TV programme

Add others that might inspire the group.

WHAT TO DO

Divide people into teams representing different organizations. Ask someone from each team to draw a card out of the hat. Then ask:

Thinking about your organization, if it were a [whatever is on the card]:

1. *Which would it be?*

2. *Why would it be that one?*

⠿ DISCUSSION

Ask someone from each team to feed back what they have chosen and why they have chosen it. As people talk, capture the different values emerging on a board at the front. For example, they might be using words that reflect values, such as 'exciting', 'cool', 'trustworthy' or 'serious'. Other words might be 'welcoming' or 'hardworking'.

Once you have lots of words on the board, ask each team to use the words to write a statement of core brand values setting out what the organization believes in and cares about.

Alternatively, use different words as a starting point for thinking about the positive and negative aspects of how the organization is seen and in turn what might need to be done to counteract that.

❦ 9.5 WHAT ARE YOUR ETHICAL VALUES?

A right to a cultural heritage brings with it a duty to respect that of others. Heritage organizations deal with a wide range of ethical issues. These include issues relating to conservation, returning objects to original owners, interpretation, sharing information, community consultations and sources of finance. The next three exercises introduce heritage ethics.

⠿ *AIM*

To introduce the kinds of ethical dilemmas that heritage organizations might need to deal with.

⠿ *WHAT TO DO*

Describe the following scenario, or develop one that is specific to your organization:

> *You are the director of a museum with an important collection of Aboriginal material. An Aboriginal community have asked you to help them repatriate a very famous set of ancestral remains. The scientists who have studied those remains feel strongly that these represent important knowledge and in the future have the potential to change our understanding of human evolution. The Aboriginal community feel that their ancestors deserve proper and respectful treatment and should be reburied in a place that has strong cultural and historical meaning.*

Divide people into two teams – one representing the Aboriginal community; the other the scientific community. Ask each team to present you with the arguments for their recommended course of action.

⠿ *DISCUSSION*

Is this a simple choice between heritage and people – that is, the preservation of the scientific value of the heritage vs the wishes of the community? Which is right and which is wrong?

⸙ 9.6 HERITAGE ETHICS QUIZ

⸭ *AIM*

To explore individual approaches to heritage ethics.

⸭ *PREPARATION*

You will need a written quiz with a series of ethical heritage dilemmas. Either use the quiz set out here or prepare your own in advance:

Would you do it? – Answer yes or no

1. You are an archaeologist working for a developer who wants you to downplay the significance of a site in order to allow for more development.

2. You are a curator and your museum director wants to acquire an object that may have been stolen.

3. You are a heritage consultant working for a mining company. If the mine goes ahead, it will destroy a lot of heritage, but your firm will get the contract to excavate it and they will also fund a local health clinic.

4. One of your major donors wants to fund you to restore a historic house to a particular period and colour scheme for which there is no evidence at all, but the roof needs repair and the donor will fund it if you do as they ask.

5. A metal detectorist has told you about an important find on the condition that you do not divulge it.

6. The construction project is over time and over budget, and on the last day you find some human remains in the trench. Your boss asks you to ignore them.

7. Your historical research has uncovered a story that challenges the orthodox interpretation of a site, but presenting it will upset the local community. You have been asked not to include it in a new exhibition.

8. An Indigenous group have approached your museum to return a series of paintings, but your board is refusing to do so, as they say that the group have not demonstrated a sufficiently strong connection to the artworks.

9. Your latest exhibition includes the work of a well-known graffiti artist – the local council wants you to close down the exhibition as it is having a crackdown on graffiti.

WHAT TO DO

Hand out copies of the quiz. Ask everyone to fill it in individually with a simple 'yes' or 'no' to each dilemma. Do not put names on the sheets or identify them in any way. Collect the sheets. Shuffle the sheets and then give one to each person. Go through each question and ask how many people answered yes (using the anonymous quiz sheets) and how many 'no' for each issue.

DISCUSSION

Is there a lot of variation in the room? Were people able to answer 'yes' or 'no' to each question, or was it more complicated?

VARIATION

Answer the questions on behalf of your organization. Is there a difference between your answers and what you think your organization would do?

⣿ 9.7 DEALING WITH DILEMMAS – DEVELOP A CODE OF CONDUCT

A set of ethical principles is another way to express organizational values. Ethical principles might cover behaviours or conduct and aspirations. Ethical conflicts often arise in heritage practice as a result of conflicting values.

There are various sets of principles that guide the way we look after heritage, such as the European heritage charters and conventions, or professional codes of conduct. Some cover the philosophical ideas that underpin heritage practice; others how people should behave as members of a profession.

This activity involves drafting an outline of a code of conduct that sets out how an organization might behave when faced with ethical issues. It follows on from many of the other activities in this book and works best with a diverse group who have had to deal with tricky issues, whether in heritage practice or elsewhere, as they will know that it is easier to write a code of conduct than implement one.

This activity is divided into two parts. The first part involves thinking about a specific ethical dilemma that your group might face (or have faced) in dealing with heritage; the second part involves extracting a set of general ethical principles from that.

⣿ AIM

To use an example of a heritage dilemma in order to develop an ethical code of conduct to help a heritage organization deal with conflicting values.

⣿ PREPARATION

Start with an example of an ethical dilemma that the organization has faced or is likely to face in the future. Use one of the examples from the previous exercises or adapt one of these:

- You are working for an organization who is advising the government on a new road scheme. A report shows that there is little if any archaeological evidence along the line of the proposed road, but your research suggests that an important site will be destroyed. The Minister of Transport wants to make an announcement tomorrow that the road scheme will go ahead along this route and has asked your organization to support him.

- You are responsible for an important 1930s building. One of your major donors – the son of the original architect – wants to fund you to repair and repaint the building. He has chosen a colour scheme that he insists is correct, but you have scientific evidence that suggests that this scheme was never used by his father. He is also offering to fund a major new acquisition for your museum.

- You work for a museum. A group of volunteers have done a huge amount to help your museum, but they are increasingly at odds with the organization and have actively criticized you in public and in the media. You are also worried about the way they are managed.

- You are a consultant who is preparing a new conservation management plan for an important heritage place and have been asked to undertake a consultation. Two different groups claim a strong connection with the site, as well as a group of New Age spiritualists and a local archaeological society. They each dispute each other's 'right' to a connection with the place, and each wants to influence the future management of the site.

WHAT TO DO

Tell the teams:

> *You are the director of the organization that is facing a major dilemma. Rather than asking you to solve this issue, your board has asked you to use your experience in values-based heritage practice to prepare a code of conduct for the organization.*

The focus is not what people are going to *do* about the issue but how they should *behave* in setting about finding a solution. Teams should start by identifying the different issues that they might need to work through in order to tackle the heritage dilemma, asking such questions as:

- Who needs to be involved in finding a solution?
- What might be important or of value to them?
- How do they need to be involved?
- What activities might need to happen?
- How will you deal with different perspectives when they arise?
- How will you ensure transparency in decision-making?
- What information may need to be shared?
- How should they behave in solving this problem?

Once they have done this, ask the teams to share their thoughts. What are the common themes that have emerged? What are the ethical implications of values-based practice?

The next step depends on the size of your group. Either working collectively or in teams, ask the group to turn these discussion points into an outline code of conduct or set of principles for dealing with conflicting values in heritage. What topics should the code cover? And what should it say?

DISCUSSION

Explore issues such as who has the right to speak for different types of heritage. How do heritage practitioners need to behave and what responsibilities do they have? How do you deal with different perspectives? What issues do you face around information sharing? Also, consider:

- What does professional competence mean for heritage? What skills does a practitioner need?
- What are the ethics of community engagement? What responsibilities does the practitioner have towards communities?

- What ethical duties do practitioners have towards each other?
- What is the ethical responsibility of a practitioner to the resource (i.e. cultural heritage assets)?
- What is a good heritage decision?
- What public responsibilities are there in relation to heritage interpretation? Publication? Making information available?

⁙

VARIATION

There are a range of organizations who represent cultural heritage professions, such as the International Council on Museums (ICOM), or UK organizations such as the Chartered Institute for Field Archaeologists. Most such organizations will have written professional ethical standards and guidelines.

This activity simply asks a group to review an example of a code of conduct and to apply those principles to one of the dilemmas set out above. In advance, you will need to obtain a copy of a relevant code of conduct. The choice will depend upon who is in the group you are working with. Ask teams to look at a heritage dilemma and explore how applying the principles set out in the Code might dictate how the dilemma might be addressed.

As an alternative activity, why not use 'Through the Lens of Value and Significance' (4.9) to see if you can identify the values that underpin the code?

9.8 TELL THE STORY OF YOUR ORGANIZATION – MAP A THEORY OF CHANGE

Another way of thinking about how an organization creates value is to create a 'Theory of Change' model. Put simply, this involves articulating the difference that an organization is seeking to achieve and then working backwards to sort out what needs to be in place to make that happen. Essentially, you are telling the 'story' of what you are trying to do and how you do it. This activity is different from writing a set of aims and objectives or a vision statement, as it encourages people to think about the connections between the things that an organization does and the world beyond it.

Use this exercise for an organization as a whole or, to make it simpler, use it to focus on a particular bit of what the organization does, such as a grant programme, an activity such as an exhibition or a specific project.

AIM

To map the difference that an organization seeks to achieve, using the idea of 'Theory of Change'.

PREPARATION

A stack of A4 card and some felt-tip pens. If possible, cut out some large arrows with space to write on them (or provide scissors and additional pieces of card). You will need space to lay out the cards and arrows, such as a large table or the floor.

WHAT TO DO

For each step, ask teams to jot their answers down on paper. Afterwards, they should put each idea onto a piece of card that can then be laid out on the table or floor. Start by asking:

> *What is the purpose of your organization, and what does it seek to achieve? Think about what difference you want to make. Note it down on a sheet of paper.*

Next:

> *Work backwards from the purpose of the organization and identify the things that have to happen to achieve that. What are the preconditions for that to happen? What resources are available to make that happen? What tools can you use to make things happen? Make a list for each.*

Returning to the stated purpose of the organization, ask the group:

> *What difference will achieving that make to the wider world? Think about some of the outcomes that the organization seeks to achieve as a result of its core purpose. For a museum, these might be outcomes for visitors, for collections and perhaps for wider society.*

Ask teams to create a set of cards as a starting point for mapping a 'Theory of Change', using the notes or the lists they have drawn up. For example: 'look after collections', 'apply legislation', 'fundraise' or 'engage with audiences'.

The cards should then be put into groups – these could be 'resources', 'inputs', 'activities', 'purpose and outcomes' and 'impacts'. Are there some things missing? If so, get teams to create more cards. See the example below.

Resources – What are the things or people you have access to?	Inputs – What are the tools that you can use?	Activities – What are the things that your organization does?	Purpose and outcomes – What do you want to achieve?	Impacts – What difference will your achievements make?
Historic buildings	Legislation	Listing buildings	Fewer building at risk	People may get jobs because they have more skills
Community groups	Policy guidance	Giving grants		People make new connections and friendships
Heritage specialists	Grant funds	Statutory casework	Repaired buildings	Nicer places to live
Third sector organizations	Expertise	Government liaison	Greater understanding of heritage	There is less anti-social behaviour

The next step is to make a big map. Ask teams to spread out their cards on a table or the floor. At one end is 'start' and the other 'finish'. Ask them to lay out the cards in order to show how the organization gets from one end to the other – from 'resources' to 'impacts'.

Once the cards have been laid out, ask teams to think about what needs to happen in order for the 'journey' to happen. These are linkages or 'preconditions'. For example, if a heritage organization wants to enable community groups to research collections, the 'precondition' might need to be support or training for members of the community group.

Next, ask teams to draw a large arrow on a piece of card and label it 'training and support'. The arrow should be placed on the table or floor to link 'community group' to 'collections'. Get people to think about other preconditions that need to be in place for the organization to deliver the change that it wants to achieve, and create arrows for these.

⠿· DISCUSSION

At the end, ask the group to talk you through the story of what the organization does, from beginning to end. What does the journey look like? Are there things that people have not thought about before? Things that people have taken for granted but that have turned out to be very important in relation to delivering a purpose and an outcome? Has the process changed people's views on what the organization needs to focus on? Might different groups – e.g. the Board or customers – have created a map that looks very different?

Having done the exercise, do people feel more confident about explaining what the organization does and why?

⚛ 9.9 WHO ARE YOU (AT WORK)?

This activity explores the different roles people take in an organization or community group. Players adopt a particular role, and others guess who they are. It shows that the way we behave and how others react to us is often governed by the jobs we have or positions we hold.

⸭ *AIM*

To show how the roles we have shape the way people treat us.

⸭ *PREPARATION*

You will need sticky labels that people can put on their foreheads. In advance, choose a heritage scenario such as a community consultation event, fundraising event, conference, a board meeting or even a party. Give the event a job or function – for example, if it is a board meeting their job is to vote on a proposal.

You will need a room that can be laid out appropriately for the scenario you have chosen. For example, if it is a board meeting, put chairs around a table. Identify a series of different roles (architect, engineer, community activist) for each person that is taking part in the scenario and write each on a sticky label.

⸭ *WHAT TO DO*

Start by sticking a label on each person's forehead. Don't let them see what is written on their label. Explain the scenario and what will be involved, then let it begin. No one knows who they are, but everyone else should treat them in the way that their label requires. For example, if it is a board meeting, everyone should defer to the Chairman, or ignore the notetaker, or react differently to the architect, the planner, the developer or the director or trustee.

Each participant has to work out who they are from the way that others treat them. Once a person guesses who they are, they should take on the role and continue to play it. You can throw in a challenge as the scenario progresses. If it is a party, suggest that the wastepaper bin has caught fire – how do different roles react? If it is a board meeting, bring news that all of the funding has just been pulled or there is a headline in tomorrow's newspaper accusing the board of impropriety. If it is a conference of heritage specialists, bring in an angry person from the local community. As facilitator, you will need to manage the scenario and bring it to an appropriate close.

❖ 9.10 MANAGING CHANGE – MARKING PROGRESS

People respond to organizational change differently. I developed this activity for a group of people in an organization in the middle of a difficult process of change. Although it is not specific to a heritage organization, there is a connection to heritage in that it shows that looking back can be a helpful part of the process of moving forward.

⠿ AIM

To enable a group who are working through an organizational change process to focus on what has been achieved and think about what is left to do.

⠿ WHAT TO DO

Simply divide people into smaller teams to explore:

- What has been achieved so far?
- What is there still left to do?

The teams could map responses onto a timeline with 'Where we are now' in the middle, 'Achievements so far' to the left and 'What is still to do' to the right. Each team then feeds back to the whole room.

⠿ DISCUSSION

The focus should be on what has been achieved as a way of creating a stronger sense of group cohesion. Get people to think about the collective journey. What has worked well and what not so well? How do people feel about change? What impact is it having? What has been learned?

Looking forward, think about whether the original plan needs to evolve, either in light of what has happened or the wider context that might be changing.

Explore the similarities and differences between managing change at heritage sites and managing change in organizations. Does the experience of going through major organizational change affect the way that the group thinks about their own heritage practice?

VARIATION

This is another way of reviewing a process of change. Take a table or a large flat area and divide it into four squares. Ask everyone to think about the organization as it was – what was good and bad about it – and the organization as it is now – good and bad. Stick Post-it notes onto each quadrant.

Use the discussion for a review of the points made. For example – are there some good things that have been lost as part of the change process? Are there some things people are doing not so well? And what are the good things that have been achieved?

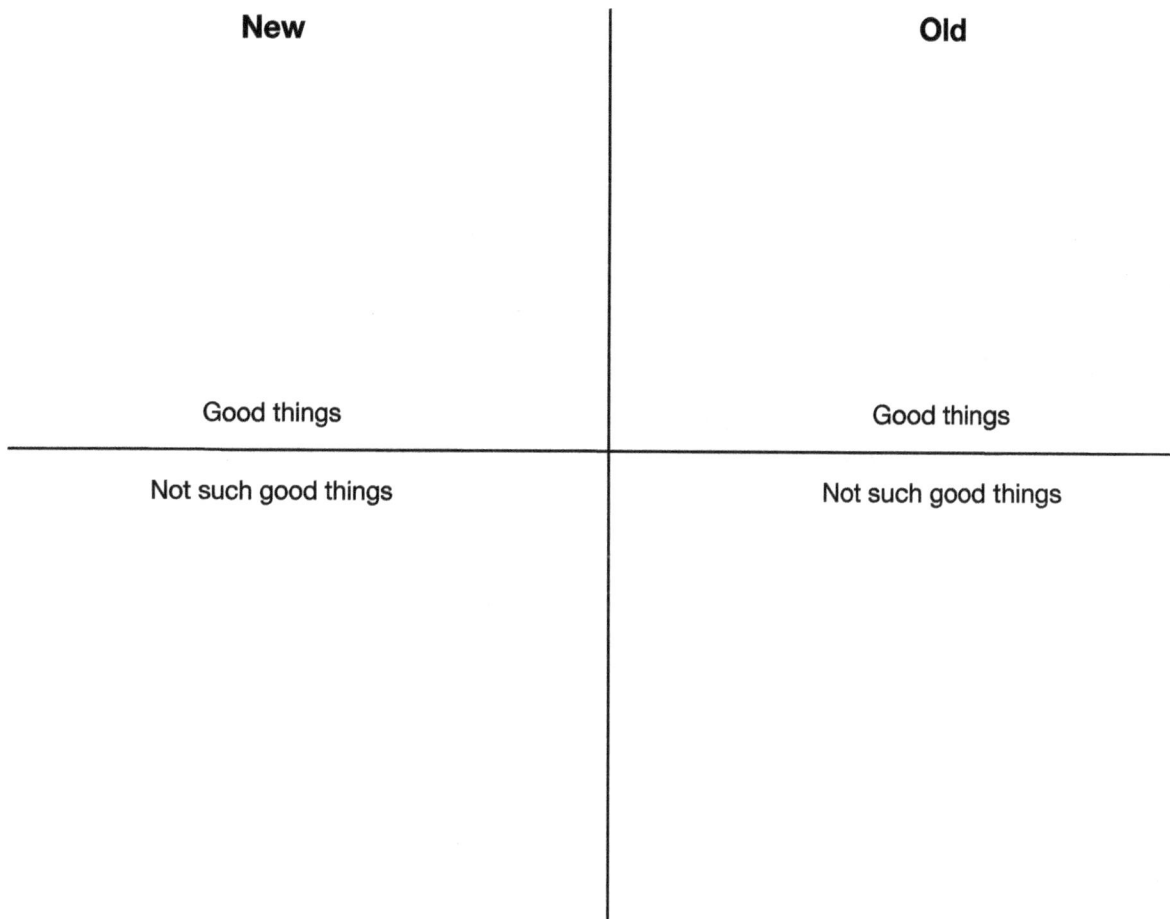

New	**Old**
Good things	Good things
Not such good things	Not such good things

❦ 9.11 WOULD YOU FUND YOUR OWN ORGANIZATION? TRANSPARENCY, TRUST AND ACCOUNTABILITY

Trust, transparency and accountability are important organizational values. This activity uses the perspective of a funder to explore them, employing a heritage visitor attraction as a case study.

⠿ *AIM*

To help improve skills in fundraising by helping people to think like a funder.

⠿ *WHAT TO DO*

Divide the room into two teams – 'Funders' and 'Members of a heritage organization'. Tell the funders:

> *You are all on the governing body of a major philanthropic foundation that supports heritage.*
> *You have £1 million to give away.*

The team will need to decide where the money comes from, the aim of the foundation and a set of funding criteria. Each member of the board can take on a character – the chairperson, the treasurer, a major donor, a banker or business executive, a heritage specialist (expand as needed depending on numbers). Tell the other team:

> *You are members of a heritage organization that opens an important site to the public as a*
> *visitor attraction. You need to develop a new facility to welcome visitors. Your job is to outline*
> *the nature of the project and then develop a fundraising strategy for raising money to build/*
> *do it.*

Ask team members to take on different roles, such as the director, the curator, the architect, the marketing manager, the head of corporate governance, the development officer (expand the list as needed, depending on how many in the group). They should decide who will present their case.

> *The heritage group need to convince the philanthropists to fund them rather than a local cancer charity. Why should they trust you?*

The funders should sit along one side of a table. The heritage group should be given a fixed amount of time to present their case – perhaps 5 minutes. The funders should then be given 15 minutes to make a decision. At the end, the funders should present their decision and the reasons for it. If you have time, ask the teams to swap roles.

⠿ *DISCUSSION*

Funders should think about the key factors that gave them confidence (or not) in the heritage group, exploring values such as 'transparency' and 'accountability'. Ultimately, do they trust the heritage organization?

VARIATION

Depending upon numbers, you could ask three separate teams to develop projects and present them to the funders. Which will they fund and why?

10

STRATEGIC THINKING –
ACTIVITIES AND WORKSHOP IDEAS

This section contains activities that involve more time (half a day to a day and a half) and that build on many of the ideas in the other sections of the book. Whilst they require more preparation or follow-up work, they can be very rewarding in terms of developing skills or thinking about values in more detail.

This section also includes ideas for bringing together different activities from other parts of the book to create a day or half day training workshop or community engagement event.

⚜ 10.1 WHEN, WHY, WHO, HOW? PLAN A COMMUNITY OR STAKEHOLDER ENGAGEMENT PROCESS

The 'Bad Fairy' exercise (3.6) provides an introduction to thinking about who your stakeholders are in a heritage context, and many other activities in this book can be used to engage different stakeholders or community groups in different ways, depending on the issue. Once you have an idea of who needs to be involved and why, the next step is to plan how to involve them. This activity helps do that, using the 'ladder of engagement' to map out how to involve different people in the project.

Use it to help a group plan stakeholder engagement around a specific heritage project such as an exhibition, a public programme or new facility at a visitor attraction, or a new development in a heritage setting. You can also use it as a planning tool for institutional developments such as a new brand, a new grant programme or a new organizational initiative. The important thing is that the project will require the support and involvement of stakeholders in order to succeed.

⁘ *AIM*

To design or map out a community or stakeholder engagement strategy for a heritage project.

⁘ *PREPARATION*

This is a classroom activity that requires large pieces of paper and pens. It assumes that the group have a specific project in mind, and have done some initial thinking about stakeholders using activities such as the 'The Big Picture' (Section 3). For students, you will need to prepare a case study. Depending on the nature of the project, you also might find it useful to refer to published guidance on project timelines. For example, in the UK, the Royal Institute of British Architects' 'Plan of Work' sets out the stages in a construction project from preparation through design, pre-construction, construction and use.[1]

⁘ *WHAT TO DO*

Starter: Define the Project

Start with the big idea. The group needs to pull together everything that they know about it – what they want to do, why they want to do it, what they think it will achieve and what or who is driving the project – are they doing it because they want to or are there external drivers?

Step One: When?

The group will need to create a timeline of the major stages that the project might go through. List the different things that need to happen to deliver the project and then try to put them into a rough order. Refer to examples of standard project timelines in order to get people thinking.

---

1. RIBA Plan of Work, RIBA website, 30 August 2017, https://www.architecture.com/knowledge-and-resources/resources-landing-page/riba-plan-of-work.

Step Two: Who and Why?

The next step for the group is to think about who needs to be involved. You might list the different organizations, groups or individuals who might need to be involved at different stages. Get the group to think about WHY each group needs to be involved.

Step Three: The Ladder of Engagement

The group should think about different 'levels' of involvement. Ask each team to:

> *Draw a 'ladder of engagement' for your project. Label each rung with the level of engagement or participation that might apply to your project.*

This is the hierarchy of engaging with people or stakeholders, which at its most basic involves telling people about something and then progresses through greater levels of involvement, such as other people being consulted, through to them being an active part of a project and even taking control of it. Ask teams to put the names of stakeholders on the ladder. Who might need to be informed about the project? Who needs to be actively involved? Who will actually be delivering it?

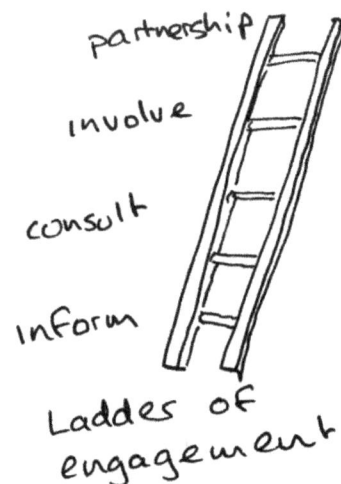

Step Four: How? Get Creative

Having identified who needs to be involved and what level of involvement is needed, the next step is to think about how to do that. Different audiences engage in different ways. For people who need to be consulted, you might use online surveys, digital consultation or exhibitions. For people who need to be more actively involved, you could put in place some workshops or other events using some of the activities in this book. The most critical stakeholders may need to be involved directly in the governance of the project. How will that happen? For example, will they need financial help and if so, how are you going to find that?

Step Five: Map the Strategy

Having thought about what the project is, what the different steps are, who needs to be involved and how they need to be involved, ask teams to formalize the strategy. You could present it as a table or as text, perhaps using the examples below. Or be more creative – use graphics and a creative layout to bring it alive!

Timeline stages	Who needs to be involved and why?	Where are they on the ladder?	How are you going to involve them?
The big idea for your project			
Develop an outline plan for delivering it			
Design the project in more detail			
Get specialist help			
Raise funds			
Design project			
Get permissions			
Make the project happen			
Use it or operate it			
Maintain it in the longer term			
Evaluate the project and learn lessons			

What do we want to achieve?

We need to revise a management plan for a World Heritage Site, partly because the current one is now five years old and partly because a lot has happened since we drafted the last plan.

What is the timeline for the project?

Ideally, we need to get the plan finished by the end of the year. The stages we need to go through are: identifying the key issues, developing the project plan, including who needs to be involved, setting up a steering group or governance structure, deciding how much we can do ourselves and how much we need help with, developing a brief for the plan, putting some parts of the work out to tender, getting on with other parts, gathering information for the plan through both research and also consulting on different issues, developing a first draft, ensuring that the right people feed into the draft, revising the plan as needed in the light of feedback (UNESCO?) and finalizing the plan. We might also need some activities or things to help communicate what is in the plan. Finally, we need to ensure that the plan is actually useful and used to help make decisions.

Who needs to be involved and why?

There are a wide range of stakeholders from local councils, who actually make decisions about the site, to staff who work there, neighbours, specialists in that kind of heritage, volunteers, some of the groups who use the site and local businesses. If we don't involve staff, there is a risk that the plan will be impossible to implement. We need to talk to local communities, as they have very mixed views about the significance of the site etc.

How do they need to be involved?

It is important to consult with a wide range of people, including the district council, the local chamber of commerce and the local school. However, some groups need to be more closely involved in the project. Therefore, we will ask them if they would be willing to be part of the steering group. That group might be quite wide – we will also need a small project implementation group, who are the people who are actually working on the ground.

We will therefore do some initial workshops to enable a wide range of people to input their ideas. We will ask the steering group to help develop a more detailed brief. Later on we will have specific events to talk to people about different aspects of the project. Whilst the work is going on, we will need to keep neighbours up to date with what is happening, so we will ask the project manager to be the key point of contact.

After the project finishes, we will have a get together to look at some of the lessons learned.

10.2 THE NATIONAL TRUST'S 'SPIRIT OF PLACE' WORKSHOP

Understanding what people care about is a very powerful way to connect with them. This activity is a full day workshop that was developed by the National Trust, and it draws on the eighteenth-century poet Alexander Pope's idea of 'genius loci' or 'Spirit of Place'.

Spirit of Place is about capturing in words and perhaps images that spirit that makes a place special to people. It should inspire any future development or change, and be threaded through the way a place is talked about.

The liberating thing about Spirit of Place is that it is free of – and separate from – the more formal requirements of statements of significance used for designation. As inspiration, here is the Spirit of Place statement for Calke Abbey in Derbyshire:

> Calke Abbey is, and always has been, a hidden house, now preserved as a rare and remarkable survivor from a vanished era.
>
> Today, visitors wonder what lies ahead as the park reveals itself from the tunnel-like Lime Avenue into open parkland. Layers upon layers await discovery with something new to explore and uncover on each visit.
>
> Whispers and echoes of the Harpur Crewe family and estate life reverberate in the house and stable yards giving the place its uniqueness.
>
> Calke Abbey is an estate of contrasts: decaying boughs lie beneath ancient trees; the industrial remains of innovative garden technology and lime yards are surrounded by rare wildlife and a colourful flower garden; the grandeur of the state bed sits amidst abandoned rooms with peeling paint and looming taxidermy; from the dark, crumbling atmosphere of the house, one steps into the fresh air and space of the pleasure grounds.
>
> It is 'quirky, fusty, distressed; a place poised somewhere between genteel neglect and downright dereliction'. In all its faded splendour it stands as a bleak reminder of, and memorial to, the English country house estates that disappeared in their hundreds during the twentieth century.[2]

AIM

To capture the values of a place in the form of a Spirit of Place statement as a starting point for marketing, interpretation and management.

---

2. This is an example of a 'Spirit of Place' statement. Calke Abbey, printout from National Trust workshop on 16 October 2014, author collection. Further information about Calke Abbey can be found at https://www.nationaltrust.org.uk/Calle-abbey and at https://YouTube.com/watch?v=UbZx9maXGxo.

⠿⠄ PREPARATION

This activity involves a full day workshop so needs to be planned in advance. Participants should be given information about start and end times, location and the programme. It is specifically designed for a particular site or place, so if you are using it to teach students, you will need a case study. The ideal location to do this is on site but with access to a classroom or quiet space as a base.

Prepare copies of the three Spirit of Place worksheets for each team. You may also want other creative tools – the ability to use photos, or paper and pens for drawing.

⠿⠄ PROGRAMME

The programme for the day can be varied according to the size of the group and the nature of the site, but this is a suggested approach:

9.30   Explain the purpose of the day. Perhaps do a brief presentation on the history of the site.

10.15   Allow members to explore the site on their own before returning to the classroom.

11.00   **Spirit of Place –Inspirations (Activity Sheet 1)**
Divide the group into teams of about 4–5 people. Give each team Activity Sheet 1 and ask them to fill it in. Ask each team to present back their ideas.

12.30   Lunch break

13.30   **Spirit of Place – Draft the Statement (Activity Sheet 2)**
Show teams the example of the statement for Calke Abbey (or any other relevant site). Ask them to draft some words for the site you are dealing with. Use the information from Activity Sheet 1.

14.30   Break

15.00   **Applying Spirit of Place (Activity Sheet 3)**
This session applies the idea of Spirit of Place to other site activities, such as marketing. This time, divide the room into groups of people who work together – e.g. in interpretation, visitor services, marketing or site management. If this is not possible, put people into mixed teams. Again, provide each team with the activity sheet. Ask them to identify three or four ways in which the concept of Spirit of Place can be used in their area of work.

Spirit of Place – Inspirations (Activity Sheet 1)

How does your site make you feel?

What do you think we can define as unique, distinctive and cherished about your site? (From your perspective and a visitor's perspective)	
Unique	
Distinctive	
Cherished	

What single words best capture your site's Spirit of Place?

What might enhance your site's Spirit of Place?

What might erode your site's Spirit of Place?

Spirit of Place – Draft the Statement (Activity Sheet 2)

Have a go – attempt to draft some ideas for a Spirit of Place statement

Applying Spirit of Place (Activity Sheet 3)

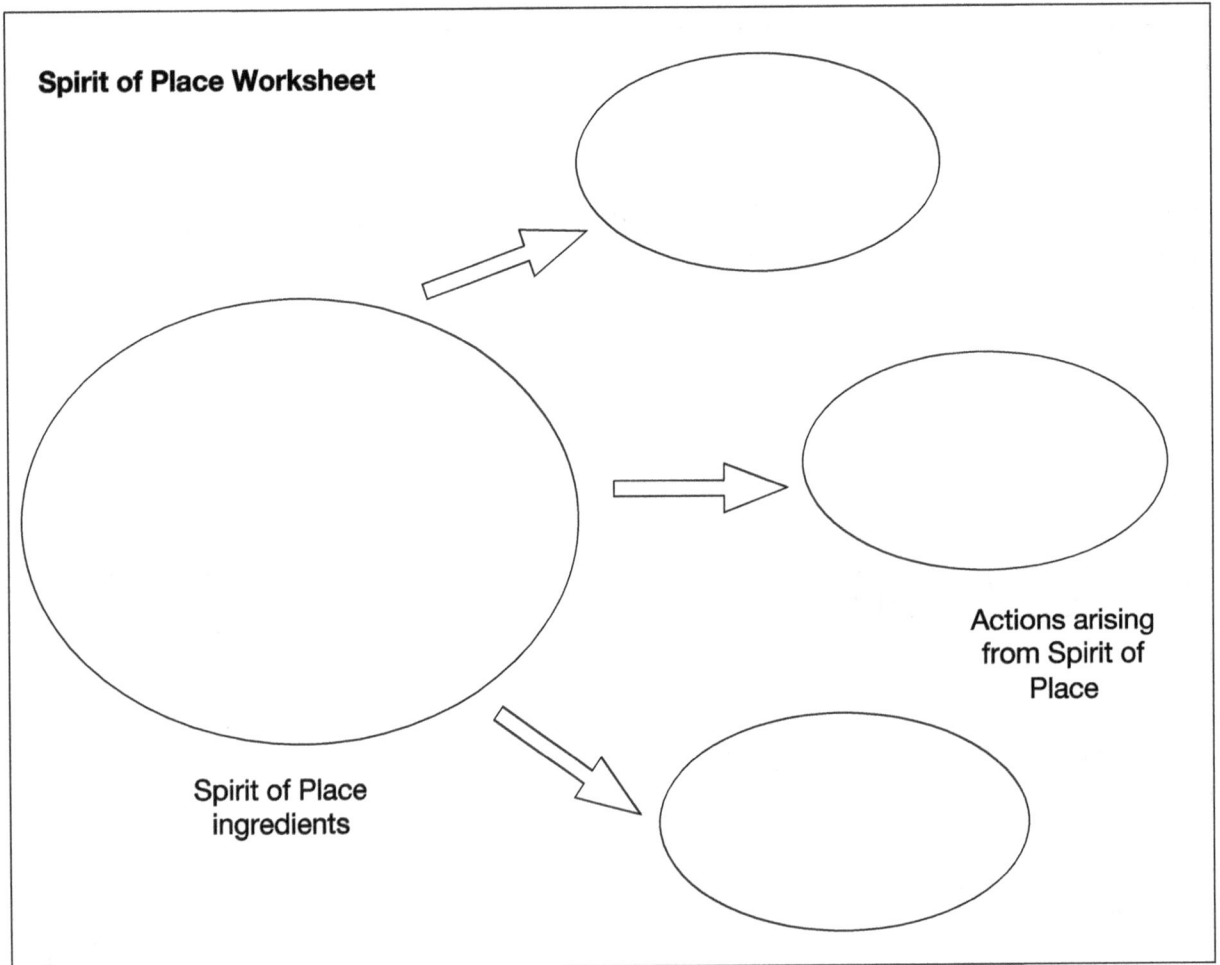

Spirit of Place Worksheet

Spirit of Place
ingredients

Actions arising
from Spirit of
Place

10.3 THINKING SKILLS – STAGE A HERITAGE DEBATE

As other activities in this book have shown, there are always two different sides to every heritage issue or argument, whether we are arguing about the overall value of heritage or debating different approaches to value.

For example, the idea of World Heritage that is of 'Outstanding Universal Value' is both a very important way to raise awareness of heritage around the world but also a difficult concept to defend when places mean different things to different people. Rather than avoiding the challenge of different approaches to what matters and why or to how heritage is managed, this activity opens up and encourages debate. This activity is a kind of heritage-argument speed dating.

AIM

To develop skills in understanding the different ways in which heritage is valued.

PREPARATION

Choose a contentious issue that is relevant to the group you are working with. Examples might be:

- heritage stops progress
- there is no such thing as Outstanding Universal Heritage Value
- the best person to define the value of heritage is a specialist
- 'values-based' heritage practice is fundamentally dangerous
- our natural environment is more important than our cultural heritage
- cultural objects should be returned to their community of origin

You can also ask the group to nominate their own contentious issue. For the workshop, you will need a large space and chairs that can be moved around. Arrange the chairs in two lines facing each other.

WHAT TO DO

Start by introducing the contentious issue. Divide the group into two teams – one for the proposal and the other against. Give the teams a few minutes to think about the arguments that they will use. Then ask the team that is 'for' the proposal to sit in one line of chairs; ask the team that is 'against' the proposal to sit in the line facing them.

You have two minutes to convince the person opposite you that your view on the issue is the right one. When I blow the whistle, you must stop and move on to the next person.

Once 2 minutes is up, ask people on one side to move to the next chair to run the argument again with a different person. For a more sophisticated versions of this activity, ask people to change sides after the whistle blows; if they previously argued 'for' the proposal, now they can argue 'against' it.

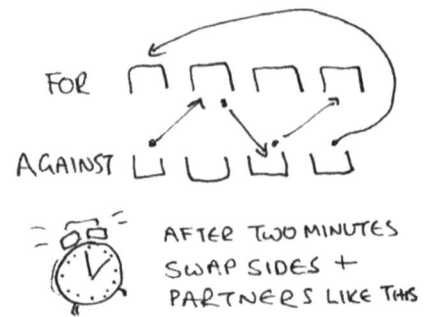

FOR

AGAINST

AFTER TWO MINUTES
SWAP SIDES +
PARTNERS LIKE THIS

VARIATION

Another way of staging the debate is to play a version of 'Argument Tennis' (Beadle 2010).

Preparation

Lay the room out like a tennis court. Ask those in favour of the proposal to sit along one side of the room on the sidelines, and those against on the other side. Leave space in the middle. As the facilitator, you should act as referee and sit in the position of a tennis referee.

What to Do

Once everyone is in place, ask each side to put up one 'player'. The players should come into position on the 'court'. Ask one player to 'serve' – that is, set out their argument in favour of the proposal. The other should respond with a contrary argument. Play it like a tennis game – with one person arguing and then the other responding.

As referee, you can score points or end a rally. Supporters can cheer on their champions. After a brief rally, ask two other players to have a go. Be strict about time in order to keep up the energy of the activity.

Discussion

Follow up the debate with a discussion around the issues that have emerged. Were people convinced by the argument they were asked to put forward? Did their views change following the activity? Do they look at heritage issues differently? What did they learn?

⚘ 10.4 SCRUTINIZE YOUR BUSINESS PLAN

This is very different to the other activities in this book. It is a high-stakes workshop, where community groups present their business plans for scrutiny by experts in the field. It takes time and effort to plan and demands that participants have a reasonably well-developed business plan for their project.

It was developed by the Architectural Heritage Fund in the UK to help groups strengthen their business plans and so increase their chances of success when applying for funding to manage and sustain heritage assets.

Whilst it can be challenging in the short term to find funding to repair or restore a heritage asset, the longer-term challenge is to develop a sustainable business model for the asset once it has been repaired. To be fair, many heritage assets fall to the volunteer or community sector because they are so difficult to sustain in business terms; if there was profit to be made they would be in private ownership!

This workshop is designed for community groups who are looking for funding for a heritage project. Individual experts with relevant business backgrounds should be enlisted to work with them to strengthen those ideas, and then join a panel to assess the projects. The reward for the winners is that one or more of the experts will then provide them with specialist help in further refining their plans.

⠿ *AIM*

To help community groups refine a business plan for managing or maintaining a heritage enterprise.

⠿ *PREPARATION*

The first step is to identify several experts who are willing to help on the day and also provide additional support to the winners after the event. They could have specialist knowledge of retailing, property operations, commercial events management or property development. They could know about business planning or running successful heritage operations, or might represent a funding organization. The critical thing is that they have skills that will help a group to reach their goals and understand funding criteria and that they will commit to providing further help to the winning group.

You will have to define the 'prize' for the winners and ensure there is a commitment to delivering it. For example, the 'prize' might be one or two days additional mentoring and support from each of the experts on the panel. Alternatively, you could arrange for the winning group to visit successful projects to find out more about what they have achieved.

The next step is to plan and book the day and contact or connect with organizations or community groups who might benefit from it. Whether you target groups or not, the critical thing is that they come prepared for the day; therefore, it may be best to ask people to 'apply' for the workshop by sending in their initial business ideas. This workshop could also be offered at an annual meeting for preservation groups.

The ideal is to have the same number of teams as experts. Teams should consist of four to five people from each project. The workshop should take a full day. In the morning, each team works with one expert to strengthen their ideas, then in the afternoon they pitch their projects to the expert panel.

In advance of the day, send participants a programme and briefing including links to relevant guidance on business planning or applying for funds such as trusts. Teams may wish to bring some material about their project, such as photographs.

⠇⠄ *WHAT TO DO*

The event needs to be run to a strict timetable and format.

Introduction to the Day

A brief session at the beginning of the day should set out the purpose, aims and programme. The experts should introduce themselves and describe what they would look for in a project. One person from each team should then introduce their project, taking no more than 2 minutes. Ask the experts to pick which team is closest to their area of expertise, or alternatively draw names out of a hat.

Workshop

For the next two hours, the expert works with a team on their proposal and business plan. The team describes/explains their ideas to the expert, who helps them to look at the focus and viability of their proposals. The plan should cover topics such as:

- vision
- capital investment
- business model
- different income streams
- cash flow predictions
- a sensitivity analysis, which looks at what happens if your assumptions change

Prepare to Pitch

After that, the teams should spend a short while preparing their presentation. The aim is to show how their project will ensure that the heritage can be sustained. It is not to provide a history or detailed description of the heritage asset.

Give It Your Best

After lunch, each team should pitch to the panel. Set the room up formally with the experts in a row behind a table and the team or their representative pitching from the front. All the other teams should be in the room during each presentation.

The panel grills the team on their project, asking them specific questions about their business model. Once again, the focus is not on the heritage asset itself but on how their proposed project will ensure that it is sustained in the long term.

At the end of the day, the panel should pick a winner, or more than one if there are different prizes on offer, but also provide feedback to all of the participants. The participants should be provided with a questionnaire to evaluate the workshop and describe what they gained from it.

🍇 10.5 STRATEGIC PLANNING – DEFINE THE ISSUES AND WHAT TO DO ABOUT THEM

This pair of activities can be used as part of a strategic planning or change management programme in an organization. They are not specific to heritage. I have used them to think about a strategic plan or to work with a community group to tease out a set of issues that might need to be addressed.

⠿ *AIM*

To identify, clarify and begin to address strategic issues that an organization is facing.

⠿ *PREPARATION*

You will need a whiteboard, lots of small squares of paper or Post-it notes, sticky dots and pens.

⠿ *WHAT TO DO*

Seat people in teams of five or six. The first task is to begin to tease out big issues facing the organization or group. Ask everyone to work individually and spend five minutes thinking about their job or role in order to identify some of the issues that they face. After a few minutes, ask people to share their ideas with others at their table. Ask each team to pick out their top five issues.

As the facilitator, make a note of some of these on the board at the front. I put each on a Post-it note, then organize them into common themes. Ideally I do this during a break as it can be quite complex. When the group reconvenes I ask whether they agree that I have picked out the most important themes or issues facing the organization or group. If so, I then work with the group to boil down each issue to a key statement. For example lots of people may have spoken about image, brand or awareness of the organization, but they may not have been clear about exactly what the issue is. Try to clarify this into a single, more specific statement, such as: 'Our public facing image is not an up-to-date reflection of who we are and what we do'. Draw up a list of the top 5–10 issues that the organizations are facing. Once you have the list, ask the group to vote on which are the most relevant to them – perhaps by coming up to the board and putting a sticky dot next to the one they think is most important.

The second part of this exercise is an opportunity to refine and clarify the big issues that they have identified. It uses the 'carousel' – a standard workshop facilitators' technique.

⠿ *PREPARATION*

You will need several flip charts on stands, whiteboards or tables with large pieces of paper on them and a whistle. Arrange the flip charts around the room. Wherever possible, I encourage groups to stand up to do this exercise rather than sit down, as it keeps the energy level high.

‫ WHAT TO DO

Use the issues identified as the most important in the first part of the exercise. You may need to try to combine them so that there are around four or five topics.

Allocate one topic to each flip chart. Assign a volunteer to stand by each flip chart and be responsible for that topic. Divide the room into teams and ask one team to go to each flip chart. They have no more than ten minutes to brainstorm the topic and what can be done to address it. Ask the volunteer to note down what they say. After ten minutes, blow the whistle. Each team should move on to the next chart, leaving the volunteer behind to brief the next team, and then add in their points. At the end, get teams to give feedback on their findings, keeping it brief.

The advantage of this approach is that teams respond to and build on each other's thinking, and that the volunteer gains a good overview of how everyone in the room thinks about the issue at hand.

I have used this activity at the start of a corporate planning process, or to identify strategic issues for the tourism industry. It is only a start – having articulated the issues, the challenge is then to do something about them!

⁙ 10.6 BUREAUCRAT BOOTCAMP – A MOCK LEGAL OR COMMITTEE HEARING

This is an immersive role-playing activity that teaches the basics of legislation, policy or process to anyone. It runs over a day and a half and takes a lot of preparation from both the organizers and the participants, who do need to do some work in advance. Participants will need to present their case, be cross-questioned and at the end a judge or inspector or the committee makes a decision. At the end of the day, everyone then spends time reviewing the exercise and what people learned.

The course involves re-creating an adversarial legal heritage process. Choose one that is relevant to the people you are working with. For example, if you are working with a community group who are trying to save a heritage site, re-create a hearing to debate the merits of saving the site. In the UK, it might be a Public Inquiry; in Australia it might be a hearing of the Land and Environment Court. As a variation to this activity, you could re-create a meeting of the World Heritage Committee, where participants present two or three projects for approval.

A huge range of transferable skills come out of the course, from familiarity with legislation and policy to the ability to construct and present an argument. It is relevant to anyone in the public or private sector who deals with heritage issues and also provides an excellent training course for volunteers or a community group.

⁙ AIM

To familiarize participants with a specific piece of heritage policy or legislation, and practice applying it to real heritage issues.

⁙ PREPARATION

This is a training course rather than an exercise. It needs to be organized in advance so that participants can sign up. Even if you are providing the course for a group of existing students, they will need to undertake preparatory work. Prior to the course, you will need to think about:

Staffing and expert assistance. The course will require a facilitator to oversee and manage the day and feedback and if possible a former judge, barrister or expert committee member who is familiar with the process and can act as Chair or Adjudicator on the day in order to give the course the required authenticity.

Filming. If participants agree, it is useful to film the proceedings so that people can review their presentation style and effectiveness. If you decide to do this, you will need someone on the day to do the filming, as well the means to film it and play it back.

Venue. You will need a room with enough furniture and space so that you can lay it out like a court or hearing, with enough space for witnesses, an adjudicator or committee and an audience.

Timing. Ideally the course should run over a day and a half, starting in the afternoon with a preparatory session to brief participants and then a bit of time in the evening to enable those who have not done their homework to complete it. The hearing can start promptly in the morning without having to allow for people to travel and can run all morning, with a break for lunch. Performances can be viewed in the afternoon.

Case study. The course requires a case study that you will need to research, edit and send out to participants in advance. The case study should involve a typical but highly contentious proposal from your particular area of cultural heritage. It could be any of the issues identified in activities throughout this book, and examples might be:

- A proposal to return important cultural heritage to the country of origin.
- A proposal to demolish an iconic heritage building.
- A proposal to build a new dam and flood a valley full of cultural and natural heritage.

Ideally, use a real case study, but disguise it by changing the names or other identifying information. Prepare a folder including information about the site, the proposal and some images. For example, if the proposal is to demolish an important building, provide information about the building, the site and the new development proposal.

Roles for participants. Each participant will be asked to play a role in the proceedings. They should be informed of this before the event and told what role they will play and whether their character is for or against the proposal. Here are some examples of different roles that could be used.

Legal Team	For the Proposal	Against the Proposal
Inspector (Chair/Judge) – ideally someone with experience of such inquiries	The developer	Member of local residents group
Lead counsel for the proposal	The owner	Heritage specialist opposing the proposal
Lead counsel – against the proposal	Local business representative	Representative of community council

	The developer's architect	Archaeologist
	The developer's heritage specialist	Tourism provider such as hotel owner
	The local council heritage specialist	Next door neighbour

Pre-course homework for participants. In advance of the course, ask each person to prepare a short written case to present and be cross-examined on. The written statement should be no more than about a page. To assist with training, also give people copies of the relevant planning policies and heritage legislation (and policies) against which to argue their case.

⠿ PROGRAMME

A suggested programme for the course is as follows – the timings are indicative.

Day/Session One – Briefing and Preparation

2.00 Background briefing

Course convenes and you introduce participants, and roles. You can also present the case study as a reminder and also make a formal presentation on the legislation or procedures if needed. For example, if the course involves a mock 'World Heritage Committee', you could do a formal presentation on the World Heritage Convention and on the procedures of the Committee.

3.00 Preparation of case and roles

Provide time for participants to work together to finalize their presentations. For example, if you are doing a court hearing, the 'for' and 'against' teams should meet and work together to finalize their approach and cases. If you are running a mock Committee, such as the World Heritage Committee, committee members can talk about their approach, whilst those presenting the case can meet to finalize theirs.

17.00 End of day

Provide time for people to finalize the preparation of their cases.

Day/Session Two – Hearing and Feedback

9.30 Hearing

Run the hearing with due formality, as would happen in real life. Everyone should go straight into character and stay in character until the session ends. For a hearing, the Inspector should open proceedings, the counsel for each side should present their cases, and witnesses can then present their evidence and be cross-examined. Put strict limits on the time allowed for each presentation, and limit cross-examination to one or two questions.

12.30 Hearing formally ends

Over lunch, the Committee or Inspector/Judge will retire to make a decision.

14.00 Judgement

Participants stay in character whilst the decision is handed down.

15.00 Feedback

After a short break, the course should convene, but participants are now out of character. The Judge/Chair/Inspector should provide feedback. If the session has been filmed, participants can be given feedback on presentation style, and participants can talk about what they learned.

16.30 Close

VARIATION

Instead of a mock hearing or court case looking at the rights and wrongs of one proposal, you could have a meeting of the World Heritage Committee, where participants bring three or four proposals forward. The Committee then votes on which should be designated as World Heritage Sites. Ask people to prepare separate cases in advance for presentation.

10.7 AN ANTHROPOLOGIST FROM PLUTO STUDIES YOUR ORGANIZATION

Organizations are increasingly turning to anthropology to help understand organizational cultures. In this activity, participants are anthropologists studying an organization. The activity uses four different kinds of artefacts to explore this culture – the organization's rituals, the stories and legends of the organization, the language of the organization, and the physical symbols of organizational culture. It helps to identify and articulate the culture of an organization, and it could also be useful in thinking about a new brand.

AIM

To explore the culture of an organization through the way it uses language and symbols and the way it behaves.

PREPARATION

This exercise has two stages – fieldwork and then four presentations. The fieldwork may take up to an hour, and you should leave at least 20 minutes for each presentation. If possible, this is best played in a meeting room that is on the organization's premises. It can be played either with people from within one organization or with a mixed group.

In advance, bring together some source material such as copies of organizational documents (business plan, brochures, website material etc.). As one of the teams will need to walk around the organization's premises, get permission or at least alert staff to the fact that this may be happening.

WHAT TO DO

Divide the room into four teams and explain:

> *You are all anthropologists from Pluto. You have been teleported to the planet earth for exactly one hour.*

> *In that time, you must do your fieldwork and collect data about this strange undiscovered tribe – the [name of organization].*

> *At the end of the hour, you will be teleported back to Pluto where you must be ready to report on the results of your fieldwork.*

Explain that because time is so short, each team will take a different area of the tribe's culture and artefacts. Give each team a topic:

Team One: Rituals and Ceremonies

This team should look at the organization's rituals and ceremonies – these are the programmed routines of daily life in the organization. They may be meetings or ways of communicating. Describe the rituals of the tribe.

Team Two: Organizational Stories and Legends

This is the way the organization talks about itself, or the stories that it uses. They may be heroic tales or tales that tell of great disasters. They may be 'foundation myths', which tell of why and how the organization was founded. The aim of this team is to identify some of the tribe's stories and legends. If people in the team can't identify them, it may be necessary to interview some staff in the office.

Team Three: Organizational Language

What words does the organization use? This team should be given a copy of a recent organizational business plan or other document. If you have the software available, run some of it through a word cloud app. If not, just use a pen to highlight common words used. What do they tell us about communication?

Team Four: Physical Structures and Symbols

Walk around the office. Describe the physical structures and symbols of this tribe – the building, the spaces, the artefacts – they might be the meeting room and table, the computers, the pictures on the wall. What do they symbolize?

Once the fieldwork has been done, 'teleport the teams back to Pluto' and ask one person from each team to present the results of their fieldwork.

⠿ *DISCUSSION*

What do the results tell us about the culture of the organization? Is it a happy place? Can you tell what the organization does or believes in? How does it communicate or work? Is the organization edgy and creative? Staid and traditional? Does it value its employees? Do people have a say in what happens? How are relationships with managers? Between staff?

⁙ 10.8 COMBINING ACTIVITIES –
IDEAS FOR WORKSHOPS AND TRAINING COURSES

This section contains a few suggestions for combining activities into day or half-day workshops or training courses. As with all of the activities in this book, the purpose of the event will be to help a group tackle a specific heritage issue or to provide generic training for students. Either way, structure the day around a specific outcome, offer a variety of learning styles and activities and manage the energy of the event so that people stay engaged and can contribute productively. Mix and match activities so that there is an icebreaker or introductory activity, perhaps a longer activity (some of which are best done sequentially in sets) and then finally something at the end to consolidate learning or plan the next steps. I try to avoid lectures or presentations, although I will sometimes use one at the end of a session to show that what seem to have been quite casual exercises have in fact covered a wide range of formal learning topics.

⁙ INTRODUCTION TO VALUES IN HERITAGE PRACTICE – HALF DAY

This is the programme that I use most often to introduce the topic of values in heritage practice. It covers the different kinds of values and introduces the ways they can be used.

1. 'An Encounter with the Past – Learning and Feeling' (2.1)
2. 'The Big Picture' (all of Section 3) – the set of linked exercises that show how significance connects with management
3. 'The Public Value of Heritage – "Significance", Sustainability and Service' (8.2)

⁙ VALUES-BASED HERITAGE PLANNING – FULL DAY

This is the programme for a more intensive day that I developed for people who need to write or read heritage reports, who work in councils or government organizations or who may not be heritage specialists but are working on a heritage project. The day is more effective if the group are dealing with a specific site or project, as this can be the basis for the heritage impact exercises.

1. Introduction or icebreaker (e.g. 'Why My Place Is Special' [1.5])
2. 'The Big Picture' (Section 3)
3. One of the significance activities to tease out different approaches to significance (e.g. 'Time, Space and Stakeholders' [4.3])
4. One of the activities in 'Through the Lens of Value and Significance' (4.9)
5. Heritage impact (Section 5– but as a broad introduction not in detail)
6. 'The Public Value of Heritage – "Significance", Sustainability and Service' (8.2)
7. Quick presentation or recap at the end to remind people of topics covered

THE 'HLF WAY' – NEW APPROACHES TO MANAGING HERITAGE

This is the programme we developed for the (then) Heritage Lottery Fund in the UK to introduce the basic philosophy of heritage to all staff, whether or not they were heritage specialists. It was part of the induction for new staff and covers ideas such as the importance of involving people, basic conservation philosophy and an introduction to engaging with audiences.

1. 'An Encounter with the Past – Learning and Feeling' (2.1)
2. 'History Lucky Dip – The Meaning of Objects' (2.2)
3. 'The Big Picture' (Section 3)
4. 'The Public Value of Heritage – "Significance", Sustainability and Service' (8.2)
5. 'Vote for My Interpretation Project!' (6.7)

COMMUNITY CONSULTATION EVENT

Activity 10.1 is designed to help plan a community consultation or stakeholder engagement strategy. If having done that you want to undertake a consultation activity or workshop, there are a wide range of activities in this book that can be used, depending on the specific context.

The 'Big Picture' exercise began as a way of working with a community group to capture their views on the value of a heritage site. It is a good starting point for enabling a group to focus on the value of heritage and how that can then inform the planning process.

If you are developing a conservation management plan, then you might drill down into values more by using 'Time, Space and Stakeholders' (4.3). You can then do some more work around the specific topics that might need to be addressed in the plan.

Alternatively, if there is a specific proposal or project for which you want to consult a community or special interest group, use the linked series of heritage impact exercises set out in Section 5. It is generally better to start with an activity around significance before moving on to look at impact.

1. 'Put Yourself on the Map – Place and Identity' (1.2)
2. 'The Big Picture' (Section 3)
3. 'Time, Space and Stakeholders' (4.3) or
4. 'Heritage Impact Assessment' (5.2)
5. 'Closer – Two Minutes in the Lift with the Mayor' (8.8)

TRAINING DAY ON ACCESS TO HERITAGE SITES

I used this day workshop to train staff in a grants organization to review proposals for projects to improve access to heritage. It would also be useful for anyone developing or designing a heritage project to improve access to a site. It is best done on site so that participants can personally experience access issues.

1. 'An Encounter with the Past – Learning and Feeling' (2.1)
2. 'Access to Heritage – We All Experience Barriers' (6.2)
3. 'Try It for Yourself – Experiencing Barriers' (on site) (6.3)
4. 'Review a Heritage Report' (using an access statement) (4.9.3)

You could conclude the day by thinking about the ethical issues involved in improving access, perhaps drawing on 9.5, 'What Are Your Ethical Values', or 9.7, 'Dealing with Dilemmas'.

GLOSSARY

Unless stated otherwise, the activities in this book are designed to be used with any type of heritage – natural or cultural, tangible or intangible. They are also designed for a range of different people and professions. Rather than explaining that each time, the following definitions have been used:

Access – activities that provide people with intellectual, financial or physical access to heritage assets.

Citizen science – activities to involve non-specialists (who may nevertheless have particular knowledge) in heritage investigation and recording, such as species identification, archaeological excavation or metal detecting.

Community leader – anyone in a recognized position of authority over a group, such as elders, people leading voluntary sector bodies, or representatives of community groups.

Conservation – the physical work needed to maintain and care for heritage assets. Used interchangeably with preservation.

Conservation Management Plan – a document setting out the value and significance of a heritage asset and how that will be retained in any future use, alteration, management or repair.

Co-production – the process of involving a wider group of people in the design or delivery of heritage activities.

Curator – someone with the specialist knowledge to select and manage heritage assets.

Designation – the process of selecting heritage assets for special consideration in planning or other legislative frameworks. It may involve a list, register or schedule. The process usually involves assessing assets for their value and also degree of significance.

Engagement – all the different ways in which heritage practitioners connect with people.

Formal heritage practice – the protection and management of heritage assets as part of the local, regional, national or international systems of governance including legislation, land use planning, taxation, funding or other services. Usually involves accountability to the public through elected representatives or government officials.

Formal heritage values – the values used in formal designation or protection. For cultural assets, they might include aesthetic, architectural, historical, social or evidential values, as well as an element of significance (such as state, national or global) and for natural assets they might include measures of significance such as rarity or diversity.

Heritage asset – anything valued that we want to hand down to future generations. It may be an individual item, species, artwork or structure, or it may be an area, landscape, habitat, townscape or collection. Heritage assets may also be intangible – such as a skill, tradition or a language. Heritage assets may or may not be open to the public as visitor attractions, and may or may not be designated.

Heritage benefits – the economic, social and environmental benefits to people – as well as the benefits to the heritage itself – that flow from investing in and caring for heritage assets.

Heritage community – any group of people with a collective interest in heritage or heritage assets. They might include cultural groups including First Nations or Indigenous groups, or groups who share an interest in a specific kind of heritage such as civic groups, wildlife organizations, rail enthusiasts, or groups who care for particular heritage assets such as local heritage sites.

Heritage disciplines – the different academic or technical specialisms that contribute to caring for heritage. Technical disciplines might include building and craft skills; archival practice; skills in the conservation of specific materials, site types, areas or items (including large technology such as historic aircraft); scientific investigation or the identification of species. Academic disciplines might include anthropology, architecture, archaeology, biological sciences, engineering, psychology, cultural or environmental economics, planning, geography, history, linguistics, landscape and museum studies, social sciences or zoology. Heritage studies has also emerged in recent years as a discipline in its own right.

Heritage elements – most heritage assets are made up of multiple types of heritage. For example, a landscape may include biodiversity, geological heritage, built heritage, archaeology, collections, traditions and memories, etc. Understanding all of the elements that make up a heritage asset is a vital first step in caring for it or making decisions about its future.

Heritage leaders – anyone in a position of responsibility for a heritage group or organization, whether in the voluntary, public or private sectors.

Heritage organization – any organization whose primary responsibility is caring for heritage, such as museums, archives or organizations that care for parks or heritage sites, as well as organizations involved in regulating, funding or supporting heritage. Note that many other organizations may be responsible for heritage even though it is not their primary purpose, such as faith groups, businesses or organizations with property holdings.

Heritage policy – what organizations or public bodies do to care for heritage. At its broadest, policy may be anything an organization does. Written heritage policy may include legislation, planning policies, tax policies, funding policies or organizational strategies that encompass heritage. Developing policy involves an understanding of delivery, of evidence and of politics.

Heritage practice – all of the activities involved in passing on heritage assets to future generations, including engaging with people, conservation, maintenance, interpretation, research and investigation, finding new uses, managing change and evaluation. It also includes organizational activities such as policy development and implementation, governance, and finding and allocating resources and leadership.

Heritage practitioner – anyone who works with or is active in caring for heritage, whether or not it is their core business or specialism. Thus the manager of a historic hotel building works with heritage even though this is not their primary business.

Heritage recipes – terms such as 'restoration', 'reconstruction', 'replication', which encompass a particular approach to conserving heritage assets. They can be highly controversial. They are generally redundant within a values-based approach to conservation, although aspects can be used as part of a mitigation strategy.

Heritage skills – the skills needed by heritage practitioners. These may range from technical and craft skills, to skills in research and investigation, to operational skills. Heritage practice also requires analytical and diagnostic skills and skills in engaging with people.

Heritage specialist – anyone with particular knowledge of, or skills relating to, natural or cultural heritage assets. They may be a community leader, academic, professional or work in a voluntary capacity.

Heritage values – the different ways in which people might value or ascribe meaning or importance to a heritage asset. These include a narrow range of values that justify designation, as well as the wider range of values that people may ascribe to assets as a basis for future preservation. They are distinct from heritage benefits.

Historic environment – the physical remains of the past that are all around us, including buildings, objects and landscapes whether buried or above ground. There are intangible aspects to the historic environment, including memories, traditions, language and associations.

Impact assessment – the process of understanding the positive and negative impacts of proposed change on a heritage asset, and exploring ways in which to avoid or mitigate any potential negative effects.

Intangible heritage asset – a heritage asset that does not have a physical dimension, such as a language, music, dance, tradition, craft skill or other form of knowledge. These assets may be captured in physical form such as a digital or other record, or notation.

Integrated approach – working in a way that integrates heritage issues into other disciplines or areas, such as health, arts, decarbonization or education.

Interpretation – all of the activities involved in enabling people to discover and learn about heritage, from exhibitions, websites and books through to activities such as public programmes or events.

Involvement – projects or activities that actively involve people in heritage practice, such as volunteering, co-design or citizen science.

Maintenance – the day-to-day care of heritage assets, including preventative work and minor and routine repairs.

Management – all of the activities needed to sustain a heritage asset in the future. Management goes beyond physical repair or conservation to include future uses, interpretation, public engagement, commercial activities and a wide range of other activities.

Mitigation – action to avoid or reduce the potential negative impacts of a new proposal on a heritage asset. It might involve new design, avoiding impact, or finding ways to offset the impact through, for example, re-creating a new habitat elsewhere.

Public heritage sites – used here to refer to heritage assets that are normally open to the public as heritage sites.

Public programmes – activities that help people access or enjoy heritage, often at public heritage sites or other visitor attractions, such as workshops, education days, open days, behind the scenes tours, performances or opportunities to get involved in heritage.

Public value – used here to refer collectively to the three types of value for heritage – significance or the meaning of heritage assets, sustainability or the benefits that flow from investing in heritage, and service – the values demonstrated by heritage organizations.

Significance – often used generally to denote heritage value, but more specifically refers to a measure or degree of collective heritage value, often used to select heritage assets for designation. Examples include local, regional, national or global significance.

Values-based practice – an approach to heritage practice that places an explicit understanding of what matters and why, and to whom, at the heart of policy, practice and decision-making. It recognizes that caring for heritage is both a technical and a social discipline. It can be adopted for any type of natural, cultural or intangible heritage.

Visitor attraction – used here to refer to heritage assets that are open to the public, whether paying or not. They will normally provide services for visitors such as interpretation, facilities or activities.

FURTHER READING

ACTIVITIES AND GAMES

There is an extensive literature on games and activities in heritage and other disciplines, including teaching, acting, psychology, spatial planning, organizational development, management and mediation/consensus building. Here are some examples that might inspire you to develop your own games:

Games in Museums

There are some very creative game developers working in museums, such as Danny Burchill. Although these activities are generally designed for visitors and audiences they can be adapted for training or community engagement purposes.

Beale, K. 2011. *Museums at Play: Games, Interaction and Learning*. Edinburgh and Boston: MuseumsEtc. https://museumsetc.com/products/museums-at-play.
> This book showcases many examples of games in museums, including games for interpretation and learning, as well as electronic games and evaluating games. Katy Beale's website is here: http://wearecaper.com.

The Wellcome collection are developing a strong expertise in games, with lots of active learning tools: http://wellcomecollection.org/events/friday-spectacular-play.

Active Learning

In classrooms, the rows of desks facing the teacher at the front have been replaced by tables and activities. Teachers recognize the many different ways in which pupils learn and also that learning is 'constructed' by pupils and not necessarily imparted by teachers.

Beadle, P. 2010. *How to Teach*. Crown House Publishing.
> This is a funny, practical guide to teaching, which for a non-specialist contains a wealth of ideas, especially in understanding some of the best ways to structure activities. His techniques have been honed on generations of school students but work for any age. I have used Beadle's techniques such as the 'Argument Tennis' for a heritage debate.

Pretty, J.N., I. Gujit, J. Thompson and I. Scoones. 1995. *A Trainer's Guide for Participatory Learning and Action*. Participatory methodology series, 267. London: International Institute for Environment and Development.

Acting Games

Actors learn theatre games as part of their craft, but they are also a powerful way of helping people to express themselves. Acting games help people gain confidence and develop creative thinking; they also have much to teach cultural heritage practitioners about audience interaction and interpretation.

Boal, A. 1992. *Games for Actors and Non-actors*. London: Routledge.
> Augusto Boal was a Brazilian theatre practitioner who started with the assumption that anyone can act. His work is relevant to heritage because many of his ideas are around how to engage the public with ideas and action.

Johnson, C. 1998. *House of Games – Making Theatre from Everyday Life*. London: Chris Hern Books.
> Primarily designed for community theatre practitioners, this nevertheless has wider relevance. There are useful thoughts about facilitation and some ideas for games that could be used in heritage spaces.

Storytelling

The value of storytelling in recording histories and binding communities together is well known, but storytelling is also critical for organizations and places. Storytelling is increasingly used in the workplace, in dealing with conflicts and in planning. It is also a key marketing strategy. Traditional folk stories and fairy tales often link to more important issues in our lives. There is much else to learn from storytelling, including how to structure stories and engage audiences.

This website has a huge range of storytelling resources: https://www.dmoz.org/Arts/Performing_Arts/Storytelling.

Dietz, K., and L. Silverman. 2013. *Business Storytelling for Dummies*. Hoboken, NJ: Wiley.

Community Engagement in Place-Making

Place-making refers to the activities involved in managing and planning for the future of places, such as urban areas. There is often a need to involve communities and understand their views on place, so planners and other people involved in place-making often use games and activities.

Arnstein, S.R.1969. 'A Ladder of Citizen Participation', *JAIP* 35(4): 216–24. http://lithgow-schmidt.dk/sherry-arnstein/ladder-of-citizen-participation.html.
> The basic idea of different levels of engagement was articulated by Sherry Arnstein but has been adapted many times since then.

Community Planning Toolkit – Community Engagement. www.communityplanningtoolkit.org.
> This is a simple guide to community engagement, including core concepts such as the hierarchy of different levels of involvement, identifying stakeholders and identifying barriers to engagement. It sets out the advantages and disadvantages of the main techniques for community planning, including art and creativity, community mapping, planning for real (making models), public meetings, workshops and focus groups, forums and web-based engagement as well as

future scoping, citizens juries, consensus building and citizens panels. It also contains useful references including the National Standards for Community Engagement, http://www.scdc.org.uk/what/national-standards/; and VOICE – Visioning Outcomes in Community Engagement, http://www.voicescotland.org.uk.

Walsh, F. and P. Mitchell. 2002. *Planning for Country – Cross-cultural Approaches to Decision-making on Aboriginal Lands*. Alice Springs: Jukurrpa books.

One of the biggest challenges in cultural heritage management can be working with communities who have very different values or approaches to engagement. This is a guide to cross-cultural approaches to decision-making about place, developed in conjunction with Australian Aboriginal communities. The ideas in here are a valuable starting point for working with anyone, especially if you do not share the same cultural history.

Organizational Strategy Games

Good strategic thinkers have been playing games for a long time and know that the best way to engage people is by having fun. There are a great range of serious games that help facilitate brainstorming and thinking.

Gray, D., S. Brown and J. Macanufo. 2010. *Game Storming – A Playbook for Innovators, Rulebreakers and Changemakers*. Sebastopol, CA: O'Reilly Media. http://www.gamestorming.com/.

The authors specialize in visual thinking and graphic facilitation, and the book contains a wealth of ideas that could be adapted to heritage. The authors explain the underlying architecture of their games and there is a useful introduction on the theory of games and the game world. Their grammar of games includes the three basic stages of opening, exploring and closing ideas.

There are also a range of companies and groups that use these kinds of creative approaches, including 'Kaospilots', who describe themselves as a hybrid business and design school who provide programmes and teach innovative approaches to organizational management: http://www.kaospilot.dk/.

Hanington, B., and B. Martin. 2018. *The Pocket Universal Methods of Design*. Beverley, MA: Quarto.

This is a brief introduction to one hundred ways to research complex problems from a design perspective, most of which could be easily adapted to heritage challenges.

Dialogue and Consensus Building

Some of the processes involved in dispute resolution that involve listening to different perspectives, clarifying areas of agreement and disagreement and finding acceptable strategies have much in common with values-based management.

Dialogue Designer. http://designer.dialoguebydesign.net.

An online process design tool to help consult with stakeholders, based on four questions – what you want to achieve, who you want to consult with, how sensitive the subject matter or relationship is and how much time you have to run the consultation. There is a comprehensive handbook of public and stakeholder engagement with more detailed guidance on different techniques to accompany the online system.

LITERATURE ON HERITAGE VALUES

Understanding values has long been part of heritage practice, and tends to be set out in working guidance and policy documents produced by heritage agencies. This section contains some examples.

International Heritage Charters and Documents

Much heritage practice is based on international charters or philosophical documents. Values are implicit in all of them, but examples of charters and conventions that are more explicit about values include:

Faro Convention. 2005. Council of Europe Framework Convention on the Value of Cultural Heritage for Society. http://conventions.coe.int/Treaty/EN/Treaties/Html/199.htm.

ICOMOS. 1999. The Burra Charter. The Australia ICOMOS Charter for Places of Cultural Significance. http://australia.icomos.org/wp-content/uploads/BURRA_CHARTER.pdf.

ICOMOS. 2008. Declaration on the Preservation of Spirit of Place. Quebec.

UNESCO. 1994. The Nara Document on Authenticity. http://whc.unesco.org/archive/nara94.htm.

Ethical and Professional Values

Almost every professional organization has a code of conduct. There are also a variety of ethical codes. Here are some examples:

AHA (American Historical Association). 2011. Statement on Standards of Professional Conduct. https://www.historians.org/jobs-and-professional-development/statements-and-standards-of-the-profession/statement-on-standards-of-professional-conduct.

AIA (Archaeological Institute of America). 2008. Code of Professional Standards. https://www.archaeological.org/news/advocacy/132.

AIC (American Institute for Conservation of Historic and Artistic Works). Code of Ethics and Guidelines for Practice. https://www.culturalheritage.org/about-conservation/code-of-ethics.

CIFA (Chartered Institute for Archaeologists). Regulations, Standards and Guidelines. http://www.archaeologists.net/codes/ifa.

Council of the Society of American Archivists. 1992. Code of Ethics for Archivists (first drafted 1955). http://www.archives.gov/preservation/professionals/archivist-code.html.

ICOM (International Council of Museums). 2004. Code of Ethics for Museums. http://icom.museum/fileadmin/user_upload/pdf/Codes/code_ethics2013_eng.pdf.

IHBC (Institute of Historic Buildings Conservation). 2003. Code of Conduct. http://ihbc.org.uk/resources/A4-Code-of-Conduct.pdf.

NAPC (National Alliance of Preservation Commissions). Code of Ethics for Commissioners and Staff. http://napc.uga.edu/wp-content/uploads/2011/08/Code-of-Ethics-new-logo.pdf.

UNESCO (United Nations Educational, Scientific and Cultural Organisation). 2011. Ethics and Biodiversity. Ethics and Climate Change in Asia and the Pacific (ECCAP) Project Working Group 16 report. http://unesdoc.unesco.org/images/0021/002182/218270E.pdf.

UNWTO (United Nations World Tourism Organisation). Global Code of Ethics for Tourism (GCET). http://ethics.unwto.org/en/content/global-code-ethics-tourism.

WAC (World Archaeological Congress). Dead Sea Accord, Vermillion Accord on Human Remains (1989), the Tamaki Makau-rau Accord on the Display of Human Remains and Sacred Objects, Code of Ethics for the Amazon Forest Peoples, First Code of Ethics (1990). http://ethics.unwto.org/en/content/global-code-ethics-tourism.

Heritage Values – General Literature

This is a selection of the many publications that relate to the application of values to heritage practice.

Avrami, E., R. Mason and M. De la Torre. 2000. *Values and Heritage Conservation*. Los Angeles: The Getty Conservation Institute.

Carman, J. 1996. *Valuing Ancient Things – Archaeology and Law*. London: Leicester University Press.

Clark, K. 2002. 'In Small Things Remembered – Significance and Vulnerability in the Management of Robben Island World Heritage Site', in J. Schofield, W.G. Johnson and C.M. Beck (eds), *Materiel Culture*. One World Archaeology. London: Routledge, pp. 266–80.

Clark, K. (ed.). 2006. *Capturing the Public Value of Heritage: Proceedings of the London Conference*. London: English Heritage.

Cooper, M. 1995. *Managing Archaeology*. London: Routledge.

Darvill, T.C., C. Mathers and B. Little (eds). 2005. *Heritage of Value, Archaeology of Renown: Reshaping archaeological assessment and significance*. Miami: University of Florida Press.

Fairclough, G. (ed.). 2007. *The Heritage Reader*. New York: Routledge.

Hall, S. 2005. 'Un-settling the Heritage: Re-imagining the Post-nation', in *The Politics of Heritage: The Legacies of 'Race'*. Oxon: Routledge, pp. 23–35.

Messenger, P., and G. Smith. 2014. *Cultural Heritage Management: A Global Perspective*. Tampa, FL: University Press of Florida.

Read, P. 1996. *Returning to Nothing – The Meaning of Lost Places*. Cambridge: Cambridge University Press.

Smith, G., P. Messenger and H. Soderland. 2009. *Heritage Values in Contemporary Society*. Walnut Creek, CA: Left Coast Press.

Stipe, R. (ed.). 2003. *A Richer Heritage – Historic Preservation in the Twenty First Century*. University of North Carolina Press.

Please note that I am acutely aware that this selection does not do justice to the growing field of critical heritage studies which has emerged during the writing of this book. Further information and resources can be obtained from the Association of Critical Heritage Studies: https://www.criticalheritagestudies.org/achs-2020-futures. The International Journal of Heritage Studies can be found here: https://www.tandfonline.com/toc/rjhs20/current.

Values in Site Management Planning – Statements of Significance and Conservation/Management Plans

Here are some examples of sources that show how an explicit understanding of heritage values can be applied to practical decision-making in heritage management. The main tools have been statements of significance (in museums), conservation management plans or statements (in Australia and the UK), Commemorative Integrity Statements (in Canada) and in the US, National Park Plans are based on Foundation Documents that include significance.

Caple, C. 2000. *Conservation Skills: Judgement, Method and Decision Making*. London: Routledge.

Clark, K. 2001. *Informed Conservation: Understanding Historic Buildings and their Landscapes*. London: English Heritage.

Clark, K. (ed.). 1999. *Conservation Plans in Action: Proceedings of the Oxford Conference*. London: English Heritage.

English Heritage. 2008. *Conservation Principles, Policies and Guidance for the Sustainable Management of the Historic Environment*. https://historicengland.org.uk/images-books/publications/conservation-principles-sustainable-management-historic-environment/.

Heritage Lottery Fund. 2006. *Conservation Management Plans*. http://www.academia.edu/3639647/Conservation_Management_Plans_-_Original_HLF_Guidance.

Heritage Victoria. *Conservation Management Plans: Managing Heritage Places - A Guide*. Melbourne: Heritage Council of Victoria. https://www.heritage.vic.gov.au/research-and-publications/conservation-management-plans.

Hill, R., F. Walsh, J. Davies and M. Sandford. 2011. *Our Country Our Way - Guidelines for Australian Indigenous Protected Area Management Plans*. Canberra: Australian Government. https://www.iucn.org/content/our-country-our-way-guidelines-australian-indigenous-protected-area-management-plans.

Historic Scotland. 2000. *Conservation Plans – A Guide to the Preparation of Conservation Plans*. https://www.historicenvironment.scot/media/2786/conservation-plans.pdf.

Kerr, J.S. 2013. *The Conservation Plan*. The Seventh Edition. Australia: ICOMOS. https://australia.icomos.org/wp-content/uploads/The-Conservation-Plan-7th-Edition.pdf.

NPS (National Park Service). Foundation Documents for National Park Units. https://parkplanning.nps.gov/foundationDocuments.cfm.

PC (Parks Canada). 2009. The Commemorative Integrity Statement. http://www.pc.gc.ca/eng/docs/pc/guide/guide/commemorative_1_0/commemorative_1_2.aspx.

Russell, R., and K. Winkworth. 2009. *Significance 2.0: A Guide to Assessing the Significance of Collections*. Collections Council of Australia Ltd. http://www.environment.gov.au/heritage/publications/significance2-0/.

Stovel, H. 2007. 'Effective Use of Authenticity and Integrity as World Heritage Qualifying Conditions', *City & Time* 2(3): 3. http://www.ceci-br.org/novo/revista/docs2007/CT-2007-71.pdf

General Guidance on Site Management

Ambrose, T., and C. Paine. 2012. *Museum Basics: The International Handbook (Heritage: Care-Preservation-Management)*. 3rd edn. Oxon: Routledge.

Chitty, G., and D. Baker. 1999. *Managing Historic Sites and Buildings: Balancing Presentation and Preservation*. London: Routledge.

Mackay, R., and S. Sullivan. *Archaeological Sites: Conservation and Management*. Los Angeles: Getty Publications.

MuseumsEtc. 2009. *Alive to Change – Successful Retailing in Museums*. http://museumsetc.com/products/successful-retailing.

The National Trust. 2006. *National Trust Manual of Housekeeping: The Care of Collections in Historic Houses Open to the Public*. Elsevier.

Pearson, M., and S. Sullivan. 1995. *Looking after Heritage Places: The Basics of Heritage Planning for Managers, Landowners and Administrators*. Melbourne: Melbourne University Press.

Smilansky, S. 2009. *Experiential Marketing – A Practical Guide to Interactive Brand Experiences*. New York: Kogan Page.

Staniforth, S. 2013. *Historical Perspectives on Preventive Conservation*. Los Angeles: The Getty Conservation Institute.

Economic, Social and Environmental Benefits of Heritage

Allen Consulting Group. 2005. *Valuing the Priceless: The Value of Historic Heritage in Australia*. Research Report 2 for the Heritage Chairs and Officials of Australia and New Zealand.

CABE space. (n.d). *The Value of Public Space: How High Quality Parks and Public Spaces Create Economic, Social and Environmental Value*. London: Commission for Architecture and the Built Environment. https://www.designcouncil.org.uk/sites/default/files/asset/document/the-value-of-public-space1.pdf.

Clark, K., and G. Maeer. 2008. 'The Cultural Value of Heritage – Evidence from the Heritage Lottery Fund', *Cultural Trends* 17(1): 23–56.

Directors of National Museums et al. (n.d). 'A Manifesto for Museums – Building Outstanding Museums in the 21ˢᵗ Century'. http://www.nationalmuseums.org.uk/media/documents/publications/manifesto_for_museums.pdf.

Historic England. 2014. *Heritage Counts 2014 – The Value and Impact of Heritage*. London: English Heritage (now Historic England). http://hc.historicengland.org.uk/.

Holden, J., and J. Balta. 2012. *The Public Value of Culture: A Literature Review*. European Expert Network on Culture. https://www.interarts.net/publications/the-public-value-of-culture-a-literature-review/.

Holden, J., and R. Hewison. 2004. *Challenge and Change: HLF and Cultural Value*. London: Heritage Lottery Fund. http://www.hlf.org.uk/aboutus/howwework/Documents/ChallengeandChange_CulturalValue.pdf.

Kingsley, J., M. Townsend, R. Phillips and D. Aldous. 2009. '"If the land is healthy...it makes the people healthy" – The Relationship between Caring for Country and Health for the Yorta Yorta Nation, Boonwurrung and Bangerang Tribes'. *Health & Place* 15: 291–99.

Little, B. 2002. *The Public Benefits of Archaeology*. Gainesville: University of Florida Press.

MacIntyre, S., A. Ellay and S. Cummins. 2002. 'Place Effects on Health: How Can We Conceptualise, Operationalize and Measure Them?' *Social Science and Medicine* 55 125–29.

National Lottery Heritage Fund. 'Evaluation'. Website containing a selection of evaluation reports including economic and social impact. https://www.heritagefund.org.uk/about/insight/evaluation.

Mason, R., 2005. *Economics and Historic Preservation: A Guide and Review of the Literature*. The Brookings Institution Metropolitan Policy Program. https://www.brookings.edu/research/the-economics-of-historic-preservation/.

McCarthy, K., E. Ondaatje, L. Zakaras and A. Brooks et al. 2004. *The Gifts of the Muse: Reforming the Debate about the Benefits of the Arts*. Santa Monica: RAND Corporation.

Rypkema, D. 2005. *The Economics of Historic Preservation: A Community Leader's Guide*. Washington: National Trust for Historic Preservation.

Selwood, S. *Valuing Culture.* http://www.demos.co.uk/files/File/VACUSSelwood.pdf.

Throsby, D. 2001. *Economics and Culture.* Cambridge: Cambridge University Press.

Travers, T. 2006. *Museums and Galleries in Britain – Economic, Social and Creative Impacts.* Report for National Museum Directors Conference. http://www.nationalmuseums.org.uk/resources/press_releases/pr_travers_report/.

UK Empty Homes Agency. 2008. 'New Tricks with Old Bricks: How Reusing Old Buildings Can Cut Carbon Emissions'. Retrieved 23 September 2011 from http://emptyhomes.com.

Values in Organizations

Professor Mark Moore is one of a number of writers looking at how organizations create value. These are general resources and not specific to heritage.

Barrett, R. 2006. *Building a Values-Driven Organisation: A Whole System Approach to Cultural Transformation.* Burlington: Butterworth Heinemann.

McEwan, T. 2001. *Managing Values and Beliefs in Organisations.* Prentice Hall.

Moore, M.H. 1995. *Creating Public Value: Strategic Management in Government.* Cambridge: Harvard University Press.

Moore, M.H., and S. Khagram. 2004. 'On Creating Public Value – What Businesses Might Learn from Government about Strategic Management'. Working paper of the Corporate Social Responsibility Initiative. https://mafiadoc.com/on-creating-public-value-harvard-kennedy-school_59cf78c31723ddefeee6dc05.html.

Moore, M.H., and G.W. Moore. 2005. *Creating Public Value through State Arts Agencies 2005.* The Wallace Foundation. http://www.wallacefoundation.org/knowledge-center/audience-development-for-the-arts/state-arts-policy/pages/creating-public-value-through-state-arts-agencies.aspx.

O'Reilly, C.A., and J. Pfeffer. 2000. *Hidden Value.* Cambridge: Harvard Business School.

Posner, B.Z. 2007. *The Leadership Challenge.* 4th edn. San Francisco: Jossey-Bass.

Heritage Projects – Examples of Practical Guidance

Many national and state heritage agencies provide practical advice and guidance on different areas of heritage practice. For example:

The National Lottery Heritage Fund Good Practice Guidance. https://www.heritagefund.org.uk/hub/good-practice-guidance.

> The UK National Lottery Heritage Fund (formerly the Heritage Lottery Fund) website contains much useful guidance. Although designed for people who are applying for project funding, it is useful for anyone who is looking after heritage. Topics include guidance on building maintenance, digital aspects of projects, evaluation, inclusion, oral history, nature and landscapes, understanding heritage, volunteering, and well-being and heritage.

INDEX